# HOW TO MAKE A MICHIGAN WILL

DETROIT PUBLIC LIBRARY

*with forms*

Edward A. Haman
Mark Warda
Attorney at Law

**Sphinx Publishing**
A Division of Sourcebooks, Inc.
Naperville, IL • Clearwater, FL

Second Edition, 1998

Published by: **Sphinx® Publishing, A Division of Sourcebooks, Inc.®**

| Naperville Office | Clearwater Office |
|---|---|
| P.O. Box 372 | P.O. Box 25 |
| Naperville, Illinois 60566 | Clearwater, Florida 33757 |
| (630) 961-3900 | (727) 587-0999 |
| Fax: 630-961-2168 | Fax: 727-586-5088 |

Interior Design and Production: Edward A. Haman/Shannon E. Harrington, Sourcebooks, Inc.

This publication is designed to provide accurate and authoritative information in regard to the subject matter covered. It is sold with the understanding that the publisher is not engaged in rendering legal, accounting, or other professional service. If legal advice or other expert assistance is required, the services of a competent professional person should be sought.

*From a Declaration of Principles Jointly Adopted by a Committee of the*
*American Bar Association and a Committee of Publishers and Associations*

**Library of Congress Cataloging-in-Publication Data**
Haman, Edward A.
    How to make a Michigan will : with forms / Edward A. Haman, Mark
Warda.—2nd ed.
      p.   cm.
    Includes index.
    ISBN 1-57248-077-7 (pbk.)
    1. Wills—Michigan—Popular works. 2. Inheritance and succession-
-Michigan—Popular works.   I. Warda, Mark.   II. Title.
KFM4344.Z9H36    1998
346.77405'4—dc21
                                           98-30599
                                            CIP

Printed and bound in the United States of America.

Paperback — 10 9 8 7 6 5 4 3 2 1

# CONTENTS

# Using Self-Help Law Books

Whenever you shop for a product or service, you are faced with various levels of quality and price. In deciding what product or service to buy, you make a cost/value analysis on the basis of your willingness to pay and the quality you desire.

When buying a car, you decide whether you want transportation, comfort, status, or sex appeal. Accordingly, you decide among such choices as a Neon, a Lincoln, a Rolls Royce, or a Porsche. Before making a decision, you usually weigh the merits of each option against the cost.

When you get a headache, you can take a pain reliever (such as aspirin) or visit a medical specialist for a neurological examination. Given this choice, most people, of course, take a pain reliever, since it costs only pennies, whereas a medical examination costs hundreds of dollars and takes a lot of time. This is usually a logical choice because rarely is anything more than a pain reliever needed for a headache. But in some cases, a headache may indicate a brain tumor, and failing to see a specialist right away can result in complications. Should everyone with a headache go to a specialist? Of course not, but people treating their own illnesses must realize that they are betting on the basis of their cost/value analysis of the situation, they are taking the most logical option.

The same cost/value analysis must be made in deciding to do one's own legal work. Many legal situations are very straight forward, requiring a simple form and no complicated analysis. Anyone with a little intelligence and a book of instructions can handle the matter without outside help.

But there is always the chance that complications are involved that only an attorney would notice. To simplify the law into a book like this, several legal cases often must be condensed into a single sentence or paragraph. Otherwise, the book would be several hundred pages long and too complicated for most people. However, this simplification necessarily leaves out many details and nuances that would apply to special or unusual situations. Also, there are many ways to interpret most legal questions. Your case may come before a judge who disagrees with the analysis of our authors.

Therefore, in deciding to use a self-help law book and to do your own legal work, you must realize that you are making a cost/value analysis and deciding that the chance your case will not turn out to your satisfaction is outweighed by the money you will save in doing it yourself. Most people handling their own simple legal matters never have a problem, but occasionally people find that it ended up costing them more to have an attorney straighten out the situation than it would have if they had hired an attorney in the beginning. Keep this in mind while handling your case, and be sure to consult an attorney if you feel you might need further guidance.

# INTRODUCTION

This book is intended to give Michigan residents a basic understanding of the laws regarding wills, joint property, and other types of ownership of property as they affect their estate planning. It is designed to allow those with simple estates to quickly and inexpensively set up their affairs to distribute their property according to their wishes.

It also includes information on appointing a guardian and conservator for minor children. This can be useful in avoiding bad feelings between relatives and in protecting the children from being raised by someone you would object to raising them.

Chapters 1 through 7 explain the Michigan laws regarding wills, the passing of property at death, living wills, and making anatomical gifts. Appendix A contains sample filled-in forms to give you an idea of what some of the forms look like when completed. Appendix B contains blank forms you can use. A chart in appendix B will help you choose the right form based upon your circumstances and desires.

You can prepare your own will quickly and easily by using the forms out of this book, by photocopying them, or by retyping the material on blank paper. The small amount of time it takes to do this can give you and your loved ones the peace of mind of knowing that your estate will be distributed according to your wishes.

A surprising number of people have had their estates pass to the wrong parties because of a simple lack of knowledge of how the laws work. Before using any of the forms in appendix B, you should read and understand the information in chapters 1 through 7 of this book.

Making a will involves thinking about who you would like to give your property to in the event you die now. It also involves thinking about how things could change after you've made your will. It is a matter of making contingency plans. For example, if you are married and have minor children, you should ask questions like: "What if my spouse died first?" or "What if my children were grown up?" The answer to the question of how you want your property divided might be different in such situations.

If your situation is at all complicated, you are advised to seek the advice of an attorney. In many communities, wills are available for very reasonable prices. No book of this type can cover every contingency in every case, but a knowledge of the basics will help you to make the right decisions regarding your property.

The forms in this book are for simple wills to leave property to your family, friends, or charities. If you wish to disinherit your family and leave your property to others, you should consult with an attorney who can be sure that your will cannot be successfully challenged in court.

# BASICS OF MICHIGAN WILLS 1

Before making your will, you should understand how a will works, and what it can and cannot accomplish. Otherwise, your plans may not be carried out, and the wrong people may end up with your property.

## WHAT IS A WILL?

A will is a document in which you state who should get your property when you die, and who will manage your estate upon your death. If you have minor children, it can also be used to determine who will have custody of them and their property. If you do not express your wishes in a will, the laws of the State of Michigan will decide these matters.

## HOW A WILL IS USED

Some people think that a will avoids probate; it does not. A will is the document used in probate to determine who receives the property, who is appointed to manage your estate, and who is appointed guardian and conservator of minor children.

AVOIDING
PROBATE

If you wish to avoid probate, you need to use methods other than a will, such as joint ownership, pay-on-death accounts, or living trusts. Avoiding probate through joint ownership of property and pay-on-death accounts is discussed later in this chapter. For information on living trusts, you should refer to a book that focuses on trusts used for estate planning. *Living Trusts and Simple Ways to Avoid Probate*, by Karen Ann Rolcik, is available through your local bookstore, or directly from Sphinx Publishing by calling 1-800-432-7444.

If you can successfully avoid probate with all of your property (and do not need to designate a guardian or conservator for any minor children), then you may not need a will. In many cases, when a husband or wife dies and everything is jointly owned, no will or probate is necessary. However, everyone should have a will in case some property is subject to probate. This might happen if you and your spouse forgot to put some property into joint ownership, you received property just before death, or you and your spouse die at the same time.

# WHAT IF YOU DO NOT HAVE A WILL?

If you do not have a will, Michigan law (M.S.A. §§27.5105 and 27.5106; M.C.L.A. §§700.105 and 700.106) will determine how your property will be divided. According to this law (also called the law of *intestate succession*), your property would be distributed as follows:

1. If you leave a spouse, and have no living children or parents, your spouse gets your entire estate.

2. If you leave a spouse, have no children, but at least one of your parents survives, your spouse gets the first $60,000 plus one-half of the balance of your estate. The other one-half of the balance goes to your parent or parents.

3. If you leave a spouse and children who are all children of your spouse, your spouse gets the first $60,000 plus one-half of the balance. The children get equal shares of the other one-half.

4. If you leave a spouse and at least one child who is *not* your spouse's child, then your spouse gets one-half of your estate. Your children get equal shares of the other one-half.

5. If you leave no spouse, all of your children get equal shares of your estate.

6. If you leave no spouse and no children, then your estate would go to the highest persons on the following list who are living:

   a. your parents.

   b. your brothers and sisters (if any are dead, their share goes to their children).

   c. your grandparents, with one-half going to your maternal grandparents and one-half to your paternal grandparents. If both grandparents on one side are deceased, their share goes to their children (i.e., your aunts and uncles). If there are no surviving grandparents or aunts and uncles on one side, the entire estate goes to the surviving grandparents or aunts and uncles on the other side.

   d. the State of Michigan.

If you leave a wife, she will need to choose between the provisions listed above and her rights under another provision of Michigan law. This other provision relates to a widow's *dower rights*. This only applies to a surviving wife; not to a surviving husband.

# JOINT TENANCY, SPOUSES, AND WILLS

JOINT TENANCY
OVERRULES A
WILL

As used in this book, the terms *joint tenancy* and *joint ownership* refer to *joint tenancy with full rights of survivorship*. On a bank account this would be designated by the word "or" between the names of the two owners. On a deed to real estate, and often on other types of property, the names of the joint owners would be followed by the phrase "as joint tenants with full rights of survivorship." If the property were to be titled as *tenants in common* (using the word "and" on a bank account), then one-half of the property would go to the joint owner and one-half of the property would pass under the will.

When a will gives property to one person, but that property is already jointly owned with another person, the will is ignored and the joint owner gets the property. This is because the jointly owned property avoids probate and passes directly to the joint owner. A will only controls property which goes through probate.

*Example 1:* Bill's will leaves all of his property to his wife, Mary. Bill dies owning a house jointly with his sister, Joan, and a bank account jointly with his son, Don. Joan gets the house; Don gets the bank account; and his wife, Mary, gets nothing.

*Example 2:* Betty's will leaves one-half of her assets to Ann and one-half of her assets to George. Betty dies owning $1,000,000 in stock jointly with George, and a car in her own name. Ann gets only a one-half interest in the car. George gets all of the stock and one-half of the car.

*Example 3:* John's will leaves all of his property equally to his five children. Before going in the hospital he makes his oldest son, Harry, the joint owner of his accounts. John dies and Harry gets all of his assets. The rest of the children get nothing.

In each of these cases the property went to a person it shouldn't have, because the decedent didn't realize that joint ownership overruled the will. In some families this might not be a problem. Harry might divide up the property equally (and possibly pay a gift tax). But in many cases Harry would just keep everything and the family would never talk to him again.

**A Spouse Can Overrule a Will**

Under Michigan law, a surviving spouse is entitled to a certain portion of the decedent's estate no matter what the will says. (See M.S.A. §§27.5282 and 27.5282a; M.C.L.A. §§700.282 and 700.282a.) This is sometimes called the *elective share*, or the *forced share*. The elective share can be claimed even if the will specifically says the spouse is to receive nothing. The spouse is not required to take this share, but may elect to do so. The elective share in Michigan is one-half of what the spouse would have received if there had not been a will, reduced by one-half of what the spouse received outside of probate (such as joint property and life insurance). If the surviving spouse is a woman, she could instead take dower rights under M.S.A. §§558.1 to 558.29, which is the use (i.e., a *life estate*) of one-third of all land owned by her deceased husband. The following examples assume the surviving spouse makes this election to take one-half of what he or she would have received if there had not been a will.

*Example 1:* John's will leaves all of his property to his children of a prior marriage and nothing to his wife who is already wealthy. The wife still gets 25% of John's estate and his children divide up the remaining 75%.

*Example 2:* Mary (who has no children) puts one-half of her property in a joint account with her husband, and in her will she leaves all of her other property to her sister. When she dies her husband gets all of the money in the joint account *and* one-half of her other property.

**Joint Tenancy Overrules a Spouse's Elective Share**

One way to avoid a spouse's elective share is to have all property in joint ownership with others. Other ways are to set up a trust, or to sign an agreement with your spouse either before or after the marriage. (For more information on such agreements, see *How to Write Your Own Premarital Agreement*, by Edward A. Haman, available from your local bookstore, or by calling 1-800-432-7444.)

*Example:* Dan owns his stocks jointly with his son. He owns his bank accounts jointly with his daughter. If he has no other property, his spouse gets nothing since there is no property in his probate estate.

JOINT TENANCY
IS RISKY

The above cases may make it appear that joint tenancy is the answer to all problems, but it often creates even more problems. If you put your real estate in joint ownership with someone, you cannot sell it or mortgage it without that person's signature. If you put your bank account in joint ownership with someone, they can take all of your money out.

*Example 1:* Alice put her house in joint ownership with her son. She later married Ed and moved in with him. She wanted to sell her house and to invest the proceeds from the sale for income. Her son refused to sign the deed. She was in court for ten months clearing the title and the judge almost refused to do it.

*Example 2:* Alex put his bank accounts into joint ownership with his daughter, Mary. Mary fell in love with Doug who was in trouble with the law. Doug talked Mary into "borrowing" $30,000 from the account for a "business deal" that later went sour. Later she "borrowed" $25,000 more to pay Doug's bail bond. Alex didn't find out until it was too late that his money was gone.

# BANK ACCOUNTS AND SECURITIES

I/T/F BANK
ACCOUNTS

One way to keep bank accounts out of your probate estate, avoid a spouse's elective share, and still retain control is to title them *in trust for* or *I/T/F,* with a named beneficiary. No one but you can get the money until your death, and on death it immediately and automatically goes directly to the person you name, without a will or probate proceeding. This is sometimes called a *Totten Trust,* named after the court case that declared them legal. You may also be able to open a bank account in your name alone, and designate a beneficiary to get the account automatically upon your death. This is commonly called a *pay on death* or *transfer on death* account. This has the same effect as a traditional Totten Trust account. Your bank can advise you on what is available.

***Example:*** Rich opened a bank account in the name of "Rich, I/T/F Mary." If Rich dies, the money automatically goes to Mary, but prior to Rich's death Mary has no control over the account, doesn't even have to know about it, and Rich can take Mary's name off the account at any time.

**PAY-ON-DEATH BANK AND SECURITY ACCOUNTS**

Until recently, the Totten Trust concept only applied to bank accounts. Stocks, bonds, and other securities still had to go though probate. Michigan has now joined twenty-six other states in enacting laws permitting *pay on death* (or *POD*) or *transfer on death* (or *TOD*) accounts for securities. (See M.C.L.A. §§451.471 to 451.481.) These include stocks, bonds, mutual funds, and other similar investments.

To set up your securities to transfer automatically upon death, you need to have them correctly registered. If you use a brokerage account, the brokerage company should have a form for you to do this.

If your securities are currently registered in your own name, or with your spouse, you would need to re-register them in the transfer on death format with the designation of your beneficiary.

The following are examples illustrations of how accounts may be designated ("JT TEN" means *joint tenants*):

☞ Sole owner with sole beneficiary:

```
John S. Brown TOD John S. Brown, Jr.
```

☞ Multiple owners with sole beneficiary (John and Mary are joint tenants with right of survivorship and when they die, John, Jr., inherits the securities):

```
John S. Brown and Mary B. Brown JT TEN TOD
John S. Brown, Jr.
```

☞ Multiple owners with beneficiary and substituted beneficiary (John and Mary are joint tenants with right of survivorship, and when they die John, Jr., inherits the securities, but if John, Jr., dies first then Peter inherits):

```
John S. Brown and Mary B. Brown JT TEN TOD
John S. Brown, Jr., SUB BENE Peter Q. Brown.
```

☞ Multiple owners; to beneficiary or lineal descendants (John and Mary are joint tenants and when they die, John, Jr., inherits, but if John Jr., dies first, then John Jr.'s lineal descendants inherit. "LPDS" means *lineal descendants per stirpes*):

```
John S. Brown and Mary B. Brown JT TEN TOD
John S. Brown, Jr. LDPS.
```

# Exempt Property

Michigan law provides for certain property to be *exempt* from being controlled by a will. If you have a spouse, your spouse gets this property; and if you have no spouse, your children get it. To avoid having property declared exempt, it may be specifically given to someone in a will. If certain items are specifically given to certain persons, those items will not be considered part of the exempt property. If cash is kept in a joint or I/T/F bank account, it would go to the joint owner or beneficiary and not be used as the family allowance.

The three main exemptions are:

1. Homestead allowance under M.S.A. §27.5285; M.C.L.A. §700.285.

2. Exempt property under M.S.A. §27.5286; M.C.L.A. §700.286.

3. Family allowance M.S.A. §27.5287; M.C.L.A. §700.287.

Each of these are briefly explained below. These are simplified explanations. If you need to find out more details about these exemptions, start by reading the provisions in the Michigan law designated after each of the categories above.

HOMESTEAD ALLOWANCE

A surviving spouse is entitled to receive $10,000 as a *homestead allowance*. If there is no surviving spouse, each minor child of the decedent is entitled to a homestead allowance equal to $10,000 divided by the number of minor children. However, if the homestead allowance would be less than what the surviving spouse or minor children would receive under the will or by law, it will be charged against the amount received under the will or by law. The homestead allowance is provided for in M.S.A. §27.5285; M.C.L.A. §700.285.

*Example 1:* George dies with a will giving his wife $75,000. Since the homestead allowance of $10,000 would be less than the $75,000 under the will, George's wife will not get the homestead allowance.

*Example 2:* George dies with a will giving his wife $5,000. Since the homestead allowance of $10,000 would be more than the $5,000 under the will, George's wife gets $15,000 (the $5,000 under the will plus the $10,000 homestead allowance).

EXEMPT PROPERTY

In addition to the homestead allowance, a surviving spouse is also entitled to receive, as *exempt property*, up to $3,500 in excess of any security interest (money owed on the property), in household furniture, furnishings, appliances, and personal effects. If there is no surviving spouse, the minor children of the decedent are entitled to the exempt property (to a total of $3,500; not $3,500 for each child). Exempt property is provided for in M.S.A. §27.5286; M.C.L.A. §700.286.

FAMILY ALLOWANCE

A *family allowance* may also be permitted when there is a surviving spouse or minor children whom the decedent was legally obligated to support. Whether a family allowance is permitted, and the amount and duration of the allowance, is determined by the court on a case-by-case basis. The family allowance is provided for in M.S.A. §27.5287; M.C.L.A. §700.287.

## MARRIAGE AND WILLS

If you get married after making your will and do not make a new will or codicil after the wedding, your spouse gets a share of your estate as if you had no will, unless you:

1. have a pre-nuptial agreement, or

2. made a provision for your spouse in the will, or

3. stated in your will that you intended not to mention your prospective spouse.

See M.S.A. §27.5126; M.C.L.A. §700.126.

*Example:* John made out his will leaving everything to his disabled brother. John later married Joan, an heiress with plenty of money, but didn't change his will as he still wanted his brother to get his estate. When he died Joan got his entire estate and his brother got nothing.

## CHILDREN AND WILLS

If you have a child after making your will and do not make a new will or codicil, the child gets a share of your estate as if there was no will. (See M.S.A. §27.5127; M.C.L.A. §700.127.)

*Example:* Dave made a will leaving one-half of his estate to his sister and the other one-half to be shared by his three children. He later has another child but doesn't revise his will. Upon his death, his fourth child would get one quarter of his estate, his sister would get three-eighths, and the other three children would each get one-eighth.

It is best to rewrite your will at the birth of a child. However, another solution is to include the following clause after the names of your children in your will:

```
"...and any afterborn children living at the time
of my death, in equal shares."
```

If you have one or more children and are leaving all of your property to your spouse, then your will would not be affected by the subsequent birth of a child.

# How Your Debts Are Paid

One of the duties of the person administering an estate is to pay the debts of the decedent. Before an estate is distributed, the legitimate debts must be ascertained and paid.

An exception is made for *secured* debts. These are debts that are protected by a lien against property, such as a home mortgage or car loan. In the case of a secured debt, the loan does not have to be paid before the property is distributed. This is because the debt follows the property to the new owner.

*Example:* John owns a $100,000 house with an $80,000 mortgage, and has $100,000 in the bank. If he leaves the house to his brother and the bank account to his sister, then his brother would receive the house but would owe the $80,000 mortgage.

What if your debts are more than the value of your property? Today, unlike years ago, people cannot inherit the debt of another. A person's property is used to pay their probate and funeral expenses first, and if there is not enough left to pay their other debts, then the creditors are out of luck. However, if a person leaves property to someone and does not have enough assets to pay his or her debts, then the property will be sold to pay the debts.

*Example:* Jeb's will leaves all of his property to his three children. At the time of his death, Jeb has $30,000 in medical bills, $11,000 in credit card debt. His only assets are his $2,000 car and $5,000 in stock. The car and stock would be sold and the funeral bill and probate fees paid out of the proceeds. If any money was left, it would go to the creditors and nothing would be left for the children. However, the children would *not* have to pay the balance owed to the creditors.

# ESTATE AND INHERITANCE TAXES

FEDERAL ESTATE
AND GIFT TAX

Under the Federal Estate and Gift Tax, there is a tax on estates with assets valued above a certain amount. Estates below that amount are allowed a *unified credit* which exempts them from tax. The unified credit applies to the combination of the estate a person leaves at death and gifts made during the person's lifetime.

When a person makes a gift, the amount of the gift is subtracted from the total unified credit to which he or she is entitled. Any amount remaining after all lifetime gifts are subtracted is the amount that will be exempt from tax upon death. However, a person is allowed to make gifts of up to $10,000 per person, per year without having them subtracted from the unified credit. This means that a married couple can make gifts of up to $20,000 per person, per year, with no tax effect. The Taxpayer Relief Act of 1997 provided that this exclusion amount will be adjusted for inflation.

In 1998, the amount exempted by the unified credit is $625,000, but it will rise to $1,000,000 by the year 2006 (barring any changes by Congress). Under current law, the amount will change according to the following schedule:

| Year | Amount |
|-----------|--------------|
| 1998 | $ 625,000 |
| 1999 | $ 650,000 |
| 2000-2001 | $ 675,000 |
| 2002-2003 | $ 700,000 |
| 2004 | $ 850,000 |
| 2005 | $ 950,000 |
| 2006 | $1,000,000 |

MICHIGAN
TAXES

Michigan has an inheritance tax. It is a somewhat complex tax, and is set forth in M.S.A. §7.561; M.C.L.A. §205.201. It taxes estates based on a graduated percentage of the estate's value. The tax rate begins at 2% of estates valued at $100 to $50,000; and tops out at 10% on estates over $750,000. However, there are numerous exemptions, including a $50,000 exemption for transfers to certain family members, and $65,000 for transfers to a spouse. This is only a very basic summary of the tax. See the provisions in the law, or consult an attorney if you are concerned about estate tax planning.

# LEGAL RESEARCH

This book is designed to give a vast majority of people all the information required to make their own will. If you have a sizeable estate, want to do tax planning with your will, desire to set up complicated trusts, or wish to deal with any other complicated matters, you should consult an experienced lawyer. If you want to do some more research on your own, you will need to visit your nearest law library. One may usually be found in or near the courthouse for your county. Ask the court clerk's office for the location of the law library. Law libraries may also be found at law schools. These libraries may have restrictions on use by the general public, so it is a good idea to call first.

The basic laws for Michigan are the laws passed by the Michigan Legislature. These are compiled in two sets of books, by different publishers: one called *Michigan Statutes Annotated* (abbreviated "M.S.A."), and the other called *Michigan Compiled Laws Annotated* (abbreviated "M.C.L.A."). Laws on wills and probate are found primarily beginning at M.S.A. §27.5001; M.C.L.A. §700.1. A part of this is commonly called the *Probate Code*. Both sets have the same laws; they are just arranged by different numbering systems.

Another good source of information is a book entitled *Planning for Estates and Administration in Michigan*, by Frederick K. Hoops; which is

Volume 1 of the four-volume *Michigan Practice Library* series published by Lawyers Cooperative Publishing. Look for sections 6:1 to 6:344. Also, section 45:24 in Volume 4 discusses anatomical gifts.

Other books you may find include:

- ☛ *Michigan Estate Planning, Will Drafting and Estate Administration*, by Joyce Q. Lower and Henry M. Grix; Aspen Publications.

- ☛ *Michigan Will Drafting*, by Michael E. Irish and John H. Martin; Michigan Institute for Continuing Legal Education.

# Do You Need a Michigan Will? 2

## What a Will Can Do

BENEFICIARIES

A will allows you to decide who gets your property after your death. You can give specific personal items to certain persons and choose which of your friends or relatives, if any, deserve a greater share of your estate. You can leave gifts to schools, charities, and other organizations.

PERSONAL REPRESENTATIVE

A will also allows you to decide who will be in charge of handling your estate. This is the person who gathers together all of your assets and distributes them to creditors and beneficiaries, hires attorneys and accountants if necessary, and files any essential tax or probate forms. This person is called a *personal representative*. Such a person may also be called an *administrator* or *administratrix* (if there is not a will), or an *executor* or *executrix* (if appointed by a will). With a will you can provide that your personal representative does not have to post a surety bond with the court in order to serve, which can save your estate some money. You can also give your personal representative the power to sell your property and take other actions without first getting a court order.

GUARDIAN AND CONSERVATOR

A will also allows you to choose a *guardian* and *conservator* for your minor children. A guardian makes the types of decisions a parent would regarding the child; and a conservator handles the child's money and assets. This way you can avoid fights among relatives and make sure the best person raises your children. You may also appoint separate persons as guardian over your children and conservator over their money. For example you may appoint your sister as guardian over your children and your father as conservator over their money. That way a second person could keep an eye on how their money was being spent. Also, one person may be better at parenting, and another better at managing money.

TRUSTS    You can also set up a trust to provide that your property is not distributed immediately. Many people feel that their children would not be ready to handle large sums of money at the age of eighteen, or even older. A will can direct that the money be held and managed by a trustee until the children are older.

MINIMIZING TAXES    If your estate is over the amount protected by the federal unified credit (see the section in chapter 1 on "Estate and Inheritance Taxes"), then it will be subject to the Federal Estate and Gift Tax. If you wish to lower the taxes, for example by making gifts to charities, you can do so through a will. However, such estate planning is beyond the scope of this book and you should consult an estate planning attorney or another book for further information.

# WHAT A WILL CANNOT DO

A will cannot direct that anything illegal be done, and it cannot put unreasonable conditions on a gift. For example, a provision that your daughter gets all of your property only if she divorces her husband would be ignored by the court. She would get the property with no conditions attached. You can put some conditions in your will, but to be certain they can be enforced you should consult an attorney.

A will cannot leave money or property to an animal because animals cannot legally own property. If you wish to continue paying for the care of a pet after your death, you should leave the animal to someone you trust will care for it, and leave funds to that person *in trust* for the pet's care.

## OUT-OF-STATE WILLS

A will that is valid in another state would probably be valid to pass property in Michigan. However, before such a will could be accepted by a Michigan Probate Court, one of the witnesses to your will, or another person in your former state, would have to testify to the validity of the signature on your will. Because of the expense and delay in finding out-of-state witnesses, it is advisable to execute a new will after moving to Michigan.

Another advantage to having a Michigan will is that, as a Michigan resident, your estate will only be concerned with Michigan state probate or inheritance taxes. If you move to Michigan but keep your old will, your former state of residence may try to collect taxes on your estate.

## WHO CAN MAKE A MICHIGAN WILL

Any person who is at least eighteen years of age and of sound mind can make a will in Michigan.

## WHO CAN USE A SIMPLE WILL

The wills in this book will pass your property whether your estate is $1,000 or $100,000,000. However, if your estate is over the amount of the unified credit (see the section on "Estate and Inheritance Taxes" in chapter 1), then you might be able to avoid estate taxes by using a trust or other tax-saving device. The larger your estate, the more you can save on estate taxes by doing more complicated estate planning. If you have a large estate and are concerned about estate taxes, you should consult an estate planning attorney or a book on estate planning.

# Who Should Not Use a Simple Will

WILL CONTEST

If you expect that there may be a fight over your estate, or that someone might contest the validity of your will, then your should consult a lawyer. If you leave less than the statutory elective share of your estate to your spouse, or if you leave one or more of your children out of your will, it is likely that someone will contest your will.

COMPLICATED ESTATES

If you are the beneficiary of a trust, or have any complications in your legal relationships, you may need special provisions in your will that will require the advice and services of an attorney.

BLIND OR UNABLE TO WRITE

A person who is blind, or who can only sign with an "X," should also consult a lawyer about the proper way to make and execute a will.

ESTATES OVER $625,000

If you expect to have an estate that is greater than the federal unified credit (see the section on "Estate and Inheritance Taxes" in chapter 1), you may want to consult with a CPA or tax attorney regarding tax consequences.

CONDITIONS

If you wish to put some sort of conditions or restrictions on the property you leave, you should consult a lawyer. For example, if you want to leave money to your brother only if he quits smoking, or to a hospital only if they name a wing in your honor, you should consult an attorney to be sure that your conditions are valid and can be enforced.

# How to Make a Simple Will  3

Three important matters involved in making a will are:

1.   Identifying the people or organizations to get your property.

2.   Describing the property.

3.   Signing the will in a legally correct manner.

In this chapter we will be primarily concerned with the first two items. Other matters will also be discussed here, such as designating a personal representative, guardians and conservators, and funeral arrangements. Signing procedures will be discussed in chapter 4.

## Identifying Beneficiaries

PEOPLE
When making your will, it is important to clearly identify the persons you name as your beneficiaries. In some families, names differ only by middle initial, or by the designations "Jr." and "Sr." Be sure to check everyone's name before making your will. You can also add your relationship to the beneficiary, such as "my son, John Grover Smith, Jr.," or "my niece, Dorothy Jean Parker." There could be a problem if you just listed "John Smith," and you also had an uncle named John C. Smith and a nephew named John R. Smith.

ORGANIZATIONS

The same applies to charities and other organizations. You need to give the full legal name of the organization. For example, if you gave $10,000 to "the cancer society," a problem could arise if there are three organizations, one called "The Michigan Cancer Society, Inc.," one called "The American Cancer Society of Michigan, Inc.," and one called "American Foundation for Cancer Research." If you have any doubts, call the organization and ask them for their full legal name.

SPOUSE AND
CHILDREN

You should mention your spouse and children in your will, even if you do not leave them anything. This will show that you are of sound mind and know who your heirs are. As mentioned in the previous chapter, if you plan to leave your spouse less than he or she would be entitled to under the elective share statute, or leave any children less than they would be entitled to under Michigan law if you did not have a will, you should consult an attorney.

## REAL PROPERTY

Real estate must also be adequately described, although in most situations the street address will be sufficient. If there is any possibility of confusion, you may want to put the legal description in your will (this can be obtained from the deed or mortgage).

## PERSONAL PROPERTY

HANDWRITTEN
LIST OF
PERSONAL
PROPERTY

Because people acquire and dispose of personal property so often, it is not advisable to list personal property items in your will. Michigan law allows you to include a handwritten or signed list with your will. This will divide your personal property if the list is referred to in the will. All of the will forms in this book contain a clause stating that you may leave such a list. The list must either be in your handwriting or signed by you. It does not need to be witnessed, and can be changed at any time. [See M.S.A. §27.5131(1); M.C.L.A. §700.131a.]

| | |
|---|---|
| DESCRIBING PERSONAL PROPERTY | The list must describe the items with reasonable certainty. (For example, don't give someone "the gold watch I received on my fiftieth birthday" if you have two gold watches. At the time of your death no one may know which watch is the one you received for your fiftieth birthday!) |
| TYPES OF PERSONAL PROPERTY | Leaving such a list only applies to "tangible personal property" such as watches, photos, cars, furniture, jewelry, etc. It specifically does not include "money, evidence of indebtedness, documents of title, securities, and property used in a trade or business." Therefore, if you have any of these types of property they will have to be listed in your will itself. |

Just be sure that your list is kept with your will. Such a list is a specific bequest, therefore be sure to read the following section.

## SPECIFIC BEQUESTS

Occasionally a person will want to leave a little something to a friend or charity and the rest to the family. This can be done with a *specific bequest* such as "$1,000 to my dear friend Martha Jones." Of course there could be a problem if, at the time of death, there wasn't anything left in the estate after the specific bequests.

*Example:* At the time of making his will, Todd had $1,000,000 in assets. He felt generous, so he left $50,000 to a local hospital, $50,000 to a local group that takes care of homeless animals, and gave the rest to his children. Unfortunately, several years later the stock market crashes and Todd commits suicide by jumping off a bridge. His estate at the time of his death is only worth $110,000, so after the specific bequests to the hospital and the animal shelter, and paying funeral expenses and the legal fees and expenses of probate, there was nothing left for his five children.

Another problem with specific bequests is that some of the property may be worth considerably more or less at death than when the will was made.

*Example:* Joe wanted his two children to share equally in his estate, and in his will he left his son $500,000 worth of stocks and his daughter $500,000 in cash. At the time of Joe's death the stock was only worth $100,000.

Joe should have left "fifty percent" of his estate to each child. If giving certain things to certain people is an important part of your estate plan, you can give specific items to specific persons, but remember that you may need to make a new will or a codicil if your assets change, or if their value changes significantly.

JOINT
BENEFICIARIES

Be careful about leaving one item of personal property to more than one person. For example, if you leave something to your son and his wife, what would happen if they divorce? Even if you leave something to two of your own children, what if they can't agree about who will have possession of it? Whenever possible, leave property to one person.

# REMAINDER CLAUSE

One of the most important clauses in a will is the *remainder clause.* This is the clause that says something like "all the rest, residue, and remainder of my property I leave to..." This clause is designed to make sure that the will disposes of all property owned at the time of death, and that nothing is forgotten.

In a simple will, the best way to distribute property is to put it all in the remainder clause. In the first example in the previous section, Todd's problem would have been avoided if his will had read as follows: "The rest, residue, and remainder of my estate I leave as follows: five percent to ABC Hospital, Inc.; five percent to the XYZ Animal Welfare League; and ninety percent to be divided equally among my children, D, E, F, G, and H." This would have at least ensured that his children got something and would not be left out in favor of the two charitable gifts.

# ALTERNATE BENEFICIARIES

You should always provide for an *alternate beneficiary* in case the first beneficiary you name dies before you do, and you do not have a chance to make out a new will. In naming an alternate beneficiary, a couple of choices must be made.

SURVIVOR OR
DESCENDANTS?

Suppose your will leaves your property to your sister and brother, but your brother dies before you. Would you want your brother's share to go to your sister, or to your brother's children and grandchildren?

If you are giving property to two or more persons and you want it all to go to the other if one of them dies, then you would specify "or the survivor of them."

If, on the other hand, you want the property to go to the children of the deceased person, you should state in your will, "or their lineal descendants." This would include his or her children and grandchildren.

FAMILY OR
PERSON?

If you decide you want the property to go to the children of the deceased person, you must next decide if an equal share should go to each family or to each person.

*Example:* Your brother and his two children all die before you. Your brother leaves three grandchildren: one is the only child of his daughter, and the other two are the grandchildren of his son. Should all three grandchildren get equal shares, or should they take whatever their parents would have received?

When you want each *family* to get an equal share, it is called *per stirpes* distribution. When you want each *person* to get an equal share, it is called *per capita* distribution. Most of the wills in this book use per stirpes because that is the most common way property is left. If you wish to leave your property per capita, then you can rewrite the will substituting the words "per capita" for the words "per stirpes."

***Example:*** Alice leaves her property to "my two daughters, Mary and Pat, in equal shares, or to their lineal descendants per stirpes." Both daughters die before Alice. Mary leaves one child, Pat leaves two children. In this case Mary's child would get one-half of the estate and Pat's children would split the other one-half of the estate (i.e., Mary's child gets one-half of the total, and Pat's children each get one-fourth). If Alice had specified per capita instead of per stirpes, then each of the three grandchildren would have gotten one-third of the total estate. The following are diagrams of this example:

## PER STIRPES DISTRIBUTION

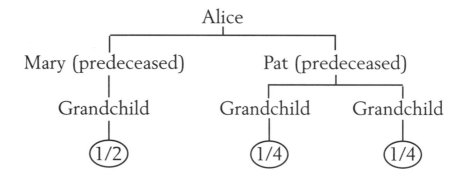

## PER CAPITA DISTRIBUTION

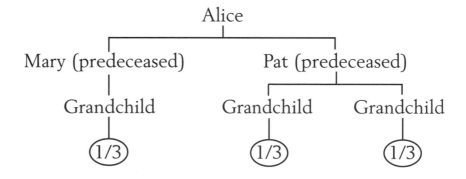

If this is still confusing to you, consider seeking the advice of an attorney.

# SURVIVORSHIP CLAUSE

Many people put a *survivorship clause* in their will, stating that anyone receiving property under the will must survive for thirty days (or forty-five, sixty, etc.) after their death. This is so that if the two people die in the same accident, there will not be two probates, and the property will not go to the other party's heirs.

*Example:* Fred and Wilma were married and each had children by previous marriages. They didn't have survivorship clauses in their wills and they were in an airplane crash. Fred's children hired several expert witnesses and a large law firm to prove that at the time of the crash Fred lived for a few minutes longer than Wilma. That way when Wilma died first, all of her property went to Fred. When he died a few minutes later, all of Fred and Wilma's property went to his children. Wilma's children got nothing.

# GUARDIANS AND CONSERVATORS

If you have minor children you should name a *guardian* and a *conservator* for them. A guardian is the person who decides where the children will live and makes the other parental decisions for them. A conservator is in charge of the minor's property and inheritance. In most cases one person is appointed both guardian and conservator, but some people prefer the children to live with one person (whom they believe to have better parenting skills) and have the property held and managed by another person (whom they believe to be a better financial manager).

*Example:* Sandra was a widow with a young daughter. She knew that if anything happened to her, her sister would be the best person raise her daughter. But her sister was never good with money, so when Sandra made out her will, she named her sister guardian of her daughter and her father conservator of her daughter's estate.

When naming a guardian or conservator it is always advisable to name alternates in case your first choice is unable to serve for any reason. You should also check with the intended guardian and conservator to be sure he or she is willing to take on this responsibility.

## CHILDREN'S TRUST

When a child's property is held by a conservator, the conservatorship ends when the child reaches the age of eighteen, and all of the property is turned over to the child at that time. Most parents do not believe their children are competent to handle large sums of money at the age of eighteen, and prefer that the money be held until the child is twenty-one, twenty-five, thirty, or even older.

If you wish to set up a complicated system of determining when your children should receive various amounts of your estate, or if you want the property held to a higher age than thirty-five, you should consult an attorney to prepare a trust. However, if you want a simple provision that the funds be held until they reach a higher age than eighteen, and you have someone you trust to make decisions about paying for food, clothing, housing, education, and other expenses for your child, you can put that provision in your will as a children's trust.

The children's trust trustee can be the same person as the guardian or a different person. It is advisable to name an alternate trustee in case your first choice is unable to serve. Also, be sure to discuss this with your intended trustee and alternate so that you are sure they will be willing to accept this responsibility.

## PERSONAL REPRESENTATIVES

A *personal representative* is the person who will be in charge of your probate. He or she will gather your assets, handle the sale of them if necessary, prepare an inventory, hire an attorney, and distribute the property. This should be a person you trust, in which case you can state in your will that no bond will be required to be posted by him or her. Otherwise the court will require that a surety bond be obtained (paid for by your estate) to guaranty the personal representative is honest.

It is best to have a Michigan resident as a personal representative because it is easier and because a bond may be required of a non-resident even if your will waives it. You can also name an alternate personal representative, just in case your first choice is unable or unwilling to serve in this capacity.

Some people like to name two persons as personal representatives in order to avoid jealousy between them, to have them check on each other's honesty, or for other reasons. However, this is not a good idea. It makes double work in getting the papers signed, and there can be problems if they cannot agree on something.

# WITNESSES

A will must be witnessed by two persons to be valid in Michigan. You will notice that all of the will forms in appendix B have spaces for the signatures of two witnesses.

Although it is not advisable, Michigan does permit a will without witnesses, but only "if it is dated, if the signature appears at the end of the will and the material provisions are in the handwriting of the testator." Such a handwritten will is called a *holographic* will. (See M.S.A. §27.5123; M.C.L.A. §700.123.)

Be sure the witnesses are not people you leave property to in your will. Michigan law provides that if you leave property in your will to someone who is also a witness, that person will receive nothing, unless there are two other competent witnesses to your will. [See M.S.A. §27.5112(2); M.C.L.A. §700.112(2).] However, if such a person would have been entitled to a share of your estate if you did not have a will, he or she may still receive up to the amount of that share. [See M.S.A. §27.5112(3); M.C.L.A. §700.112(3).]

# SELF-PROVING AFFIDAVITS

Form 18 in appendix B is a *self-proving* affidavit for a will. Form 20 is a self-proving affidavit for a codicil to a will. A self-proving affidavit is simply a notarized statement verifying the signatures of the testator and witnesses to the will. A will only needs two witnesses to be legal in Michigan, and a self-proving affidavit has no legal effect in Michigan at the present time. Even so, there are still two good reasons why you may want to attach a self-proving affidavit to your Michigan will.

First, at some point in the future Michigan may adopt a self-proving law. Legislatures are always changing laws to try to justify their existence, so you never know when the Michigan Legislature may look at self-proving provisions. If this law is ever adopted, it will make it easier to have your will admitted to probate, because your personal representative won't need to locate a witness.

Second, if you ever move to another state, or if you own property in another state at the time of death, your Michigan will may need to be probated in that other state. Such a provision can get the will admitted to probate much faster in a state which accepts self-proving provisions. Without a self-proving provision, one of the witnesses has to either testify at a court hearing or sign an oath. This can cause a delay in probating your estate if the witness cannot be located quickly, or cannot get to the courthouse right away. With a self-proving provision, the will can be immediately accepted by the court—even if both witnesses are deceased.

Therefore, it won't hurt, and it may help, to have the self-proving affidavit completed and attached to all wills and codicils.

# FUNERAL ARRANGEMENTS

There is no harm in stating your funeral arrangement preferences in your will, but such directions are not legally enforceable, and many times a will is not found until after the funeral. Therefore it is better to tell your family of your wishes, or to make prior arrangements yourself.

# MISCELLANEOUS CONSIDERATIONS

Your will can be typed, handwritten, or filled in on a form. It should have no "white-outs" or erasures. If, for some reason, it is impossible to make a will without corrections, the corrections should be initialed by you and both witnesses. If there are two or more pages, they should be fastened together and each page should be initialed.

# FORMS

There are several different forms included in this book for easy use. You can either cut them out, photocopy them, or retype them on plain paper. The forms are self-explanatory. Just fill in the blanks with the appropriate information to fit your situation and desires. The following information may also be helpful.

MICHIGAN STATUTORY WILL

The Michigan statutes now include a Michigan Statutory Will (Form 3 in appendix B) for a simple will. You need to be aware that this form is limited in what it can do. The Michigan Statutory Will (Form 3) only gives you the following options:

1.  to make two specific bequests.

2.  to leave your personal and household items to your spouse or children.

3.  to leave the balance of your estate, or your entire estate, to either:

    - those persons who would get it if you did not have a will,

    *or*

    - one-half to those who would get it if you had no will, and one-half to your spouse's heirs if your spouse died with no will.

4.  to appoint a personal representative for your estate, and appoint a guardian and conservator for your minor children.

If you want to do anything else, you cannot use the Michigan Statutory Will form. For example, you can not give 60% of your estate to one child and 40% to the other child. It would be a good idea for you to read through this form even if you don't use it, because it explains some important considerations and legal requirements which apply to any will form.

**OTHER WILL FORMS**

See the beginning of appendix B for a list of the various forms and a summary of what each one provides. You will need to select the form to fit your desires as to the number and type of beneficiaries. Be sure to check appendix A for examples of some of the forms completed for fictional people.

If you find you have a special situation that requires forms not included in the appendix, refer to the section entitled "Legal Research" in chapter 1. If your situation is complex, and especially if your estate will exceed the federal unified credit (see the section on "Estate and Inheritance Taxes" in chapter 1), consult an attorney.

# How to Execute 4 a Will

The signing of a will is a serious legal event, and must be done properly or the will may be declared invalid. Preferably, it should be done in a private room without distraction.

To be legal in Michigan, a will must be signed by the person making the will (the *testator*), and by two competent witnesses. *Competent* means they would be legally qualified to be a witness in court. Witnesses should be eighteen years of age or older, and mentally competent.

A person who is a beneficiary in the will should *not* sign as a witness. If a person named as a beneficiary in the will does sign as a witness, he or she will not be able to inherit under the will. The only exceptions are where (1) the will was signed by a third witness, who is not a beneficiary, or (2) the beneficiary/witness would be entitled to a share of the estate if there was no will (in which case he or she will get up to the amount he or she would have received if there was no will).

## Signing Procedures

Although not legally required, the best way to conduct a will signing is as follows: All parties should watch each other sign. No one should leave the scene until all have signed. The testator and all witnesses should be able to see each other and the will. The testator should state, "This is my will. I have read it and understand it, and this is how I want it to read. I want you people to be my witnesses." Then the testator and the witnesses should watch each other sign.

There are a few general rules of which to be aware, in the event they apply to your situation.

☞ The testator and witnesses may sign the will in any order. However, the witnesses must still be able to testify that the testator acknowledged his or her signature to them.

☞ If the testator is unable to sign his or her name to the will, he or she may direct someone else to sign. The person who signs must do so at the direction of the testator and in the testator's presence. This act of signing can either be done in the presence of the witnesses, or the witnesses can sign later if the testator makes the statement referred to above and adds, "This will was signed at my direction and in my presence." The witnesses may then sign.

☞ The testator and witnesses do not need to sign in each other's presence (although this would be the preferable way). The testator may sign the will in advance, and later present it to the witness and make the statement referred to above and add, "I have signed this as my will." The witnesses may then sign.

## SELF-PROVING AFFIDAVITS

Although it is not required in Michigan, it is also a good idea to have the testator and witnesses sign before a notary public, and complete the self-proving affidavit (Form 18 in appendix B). This form should then be attached as the last page of the will.

## COPIES OF YOUR WILL

It is a good idea to make at least one copy of your will, but you should not sign or notarize any copies. The reason for this is that if you cancel or intentionally destroy your original will, someone might bring out a copy and say that it is the original, or that it is a copy of a still-valid will.

# AFTER YOU SIGN YOUR WILL 5

## STORING YOUR WILL

Your will should be kept in a place safe from fire, and easily accessible to your heirs. Your personal representative should know of its whereabouts. It can be kept in a home safe or fire box, or in a safe deposit box in a bank. In some states, a will should not be placed in a safe deposit box because they are sealed at death. However, in Michigan it is easy to get a will out of a deceased person's safe deposit box.

Wills are not usually filed anywhere until after a person's death. However, for a small fee, a will may be filed with your county's probate court for safekeeping. No one has to know what you have put in your will while you are alive. Often an attorney who prepares a will offers to keep it in his or her safe deposit box at no charge. This way the attorney will likely be contacted at the time of death and will be in a good position to do the lucrative probate work.

If you are close to your children and can trust them explicitly, then you could allow one of them to keep your will in his or her safe deposit box. However, if you later decide to limit that child's share, there could be a problem.

*Example:* Diane made out her will, giving her property to her two children equally, and gave the will to her older child, Bill, to hold. Years later, Bill moved away and had little further contact with his mother. Diane's younger child, Mary, took care of her during her final illness, so Diane made a new will giving most of her property to Mary. Upon Diane's death, Bill returned and found the new will in Diane's house. He destroyed the new will and probated the old will which gave him one-half of the property.

## REVOKING YOUR WILL

A person who has made a will may revoke it, or may direct someone else to revoke it in his presence. This may be done by burning, tearing, cancelling, defacing, obliterating, or destroying it with the intention and for the purpose of revoking it. Revoking one will does not revive an older will. Ideally, the original will, and all copies, should be totally destroyed.

*Example:* Ralph tells his son, Clyde, to go to the basement safe and tear up his (Ralph's) will. If Clyde does not tear it up in Ralph's presence it is probably not effectively revoked.

A will is also revoked by the execution of a new will. The new will should contain the phrase, "I revoke any prior wills and codicils."

## CHANGING YOUR WILL

You may not make any changes on your will after it has been signed. If you cross out a person's name or add a new clause to a will that has already been signed, your change will not be valid, and your entire will might become invalid!

If you wish to change some provision of your will, you can do it by executing a document called a *codicil*. A person may make an unlimited number of codicils to a will, but each one must be executed with the same formality of a will (i.e., two witnesses, etc.). Also, if there are several codicils, it can be difficult to locate all of them, figure out exactly how each one modifies the will or a previous codicil, track down the necessary witnesses, and determine how the estate is to be divided. Therefore, it is usually better to prepare a new will instead of a codicil.

Form 19 in appendix B is a codicil. Although it is not necessary, you should also use the self-proved codicil affidavit (Form 20) and attach it to your codicil. (See chapter 3 for more information on self-proving affidavits.)

# How to Make a Living Will 6

A *living will* is a document by which a person declares that he or she does not want certain types of medical treatment if he or she becomes terminally ill. A living will has nothing to do with the traditional will that distributes property.

Modern science can often keep a body alive even if the brain is permanently dead. The living will is designed for a person to be able to state in advance that he or she does not want such treatment.

In 1990, Michigan passed a law which allows a person to designate a *patient advocate*. (See M.S.A. §27.5496; M.C.L.A. §700.496.) This law is different from a traditional living will, in that a living will was only a statement of your desires concerning the use of life-prolonging procedures in the event you were terminally ill (it did not involve appointing anyone to make decisions for you, and did not cover medical decisions or treatment where there was no terminal illness or condition).

The current Michigan law allows you to designate someone to make health care decisions for you whenever you are unable to do so for yourself (even if there is no terminal condition). In other states this may be referred to as a *health care power of attorney*. The person you designate is called a *patient advocate*. Under this law, a designation of patient advocate document can be signed at any time by someone who is at least eighteen years of age and of sound mind.

Not anyone can be a witness to your Designation of Patient Advocate and Living Will (Form 21), which must be signed in front of two witnesses, neither of whom are:

1.  the person's spouse, parent, child, grandchild, brother, or sister;

2.  the person's presumptive heir (i.e., one who will inherit from the person), or a known devisee under the person's will at the time of witnessing;

3.  the person's physician;

4.  the person's designated patient advocate;

5.  an employee of a life or health insurance provider for the person;

6.  an employee of a health facility treating the person; or

7.  an employee of a home for the aged where the person lives.

The Designation of Patient Advocate may include a statement of the person's desires about his or her care, custody, and medical treatment, and may specifically designate or limit the powers of the patient advocate. A patient advocate may not decide to withhold or withdraw treatment that would allow you to die, unless you specifically give him or her that power. You may also designate an alternate patient advocate in the event your first choice is unable or unwilling to act.

Before acting, the patient advocate must accept the responsibility by signing an acceptance provision (which is also included in Form 21 in appendix B).

The law creating this is fairly detailed, taking up five pages in the statutes. It covers various possible situations, such as:

☞ what and who determines that the patient is unable to participate in decision-making, so as to allow the patient advocate to make decisions,

☛ restrictions if the patient is pregnant, and

☛ when and under what circumstances certain types of decisions may be made.

If you have any questions about this, it is strongly suggested that you read the entire statute (M.S.A. §27.5496; M.C.L.A. §700.496) before you sign a Designation of Patient Advocate and Living Will.

An example of a completed Designation of Patient Advocate and Living Will (Form 21) is also included in appendix A.

# How to Make Anatomical Gifts 7

The Uniform Anatomical Gift Act [M.S.A. §14.15(10101); M.C.L.A. §333.10101], allows Michigan residents to donate their bodies or organs for research or transplantation. Consent may also be given by certain relatives of a deceased person but, because relatives are often in shock and too upset to make such a decision, or don't believe in body or organ donation, it is better to have your intent made clear before death. This can be done by a statement in a regular will, or by another signed document such as the Uniform Donor Card (Form 22). The gift may be of all or part of one's body, and it may be made to a specific person such as a physician or an ill relative.

The document making the donation must be signed before two witnesses, who must also sign in each other's presence. If the donor cannot sign, then the document may be signed for him at his direction in the presence of the witnesses.

The donor may designate in the document who the physician is who will carry out the procedure.

If the document has been delivered to a specific donee, it may be amended or revoked by a person in the following ways:

1. By executing and delivering a signed statement to the donee.

2. By an oral statement to two witnesses and communicated to the donee.

3. By an oral statement during a terminal illness or injury made to an attending physician and communicated to the donee.

4. By a signed document found on the person of the donor or in his or her effects.

If a document of gift has not been delivered to a donee, it may be revoked by any of the above methods or by destruction, cancellation, or mutilation of the document and all copies. If included in a will, it may also be revoked in the same method a will is revoked as described in chapter 5.

# APPENDIX A
# SAMPLE FORMS

This appendix contains examples of some of the forms from appendix B, which have been filled-in for fictional people. This should give you a better idea of how your forms should look when completed.

Where the number of pages has been filled in (e.g., "Page 2 of _7_ pages."), it has been assumed that the self-proved affidavit (Form 18 or Form 20) has been added as the last page. However, the self-proved affidavit has not been included in each example.

The following completed forms are included in this appendix:

**Form 3. Michigan Statutory Will**. (**Note:** *Page 6 of this form, which does not have any blanks to fill in, has been omitted in order to save space) This is a will form provided in the Michigan statutes, and is quite limited in what it can accomplish. Be sure to read the information on the Michigan Statutory Will on page 33 before you use this form.*

**Form 7. Simple Will**—Spouse and No Children. *Use this will if you want your property to go to your spouse, but if your spouse dies previously, to others or the* **survivor** *of the others.*

**Form 9. Simple Will**—Spouse and Adult Children. *Use this will if you want all of your property to go to your spouse, but if your spouse dies previously, then to your children, all of whom are adults.*

**Form 12. Simple Will—No Spouse—Minor Children—Separate Guardian and Conservator.** *Use this will if you do not have a spouse and want all your property to go to your children, at least one of whom is a minor. It provides for two different people to serve as guardian over your children and conservator over their estates.*

**Form 18. Self-Proved Will Page.** *This page should be attached to every will as the last page. It must be witnessed and notarized.*

**Form 19. Codicil to Will.** *This form can be used to change one section of your will. Usually it is just as easy to execute a new will, since all of the same formalities are required.*

**Form 21. Designation of Patient Advocate and Living Will.** *This form is used to state that you do not want your life artificially prolonged if you have a terminal illness, and to designate a person to make medical decisions for you if you are unable to make such decisions yourself.*

## MICHIGAN STATUTORY WILL
### NOTICE

1. Any person age 18 or older and of sound mind may sign a will.
2. There are several kinds of wills. If you choose to complete this form, you will have a Michigan statutory will. If this will does not meet your wishes in any way, you should talk with a lawyer before choosing a Michigan statutory will.
3. Warning! It is strongly recommended that you do not add or cross out any words on this form except for filling in the blanks because all or part of this will may not be valid if you do so.
4. This will has no effect on jointly-held assets, on retirement plan benefits, or on life insurance on your life if you have named a beneficiary who survives you.
5. This will is not designed to reduce inheritance or estate taxes.
6. This will treats adopted children and children born outside wedlock who would inherit if their parent died without a will the same way as children born or conceived during marriage.
7. You should keep this will in your safe deposit box or other safe place. By paying a small fee, you may file the will in your county's probate court for safekeeping. You should tell your family where the will is kept.
8. You may make and sign a new will at any time. If you marry or divorce after you sign this will, you should make a new will.

INSTRUCTIONS:
1. To have a Michigan statutory will, you must complete the blanks on the will form. You may do this yourself, or direct someone to do it for you. You must either sign the will or direct someone else to sign it in your name and in your presence.
2. Read the entire Michigan statutory will carefully before you begin filling in the blanks. If there is anything you do not understand, you should ask a lawyer to explain it to you.

### MICHIGAN STATUTORY WILL OF

Henry Edsel Ford
_____
(Print or type your full name)

### ARTICLE 1. DECLARATIONS

This is my will and I revoke any prior wills and codicils. I live in _____Wayne_____ County, Michigan.

My spouse is _____Holley Dodge Ford_____
(Insert spouse's name or write "None")

My children now living are:

Fred Ford_____     Joe Louis Ford_____
(Insert names or write "None")

Ann Allen Ford Fischer_____     Smokey Robinson Ford_____

Benton Harbor Ford_____     _____

Page 1 of _7_ pages.

## ARTICLE 2. DISPOSITION OF MY ASSETS

2.1     CASH GIFTS TO PERSONS OR CHARITIES.  (Optional)

I can leave no more that two (2) cash gifts.  I make the following cash gifts to the persons or charities in the amounts stated here.  Any inheritance tax due shall be paid from the balance of my estate and not from these gifts.

Full name and address of person or charity to receive cash gift.
(Name only one (1) person or charity here)
(Please print)_____ Detroit Institute of Arts _____
(Insert name)

of _____ Woodward Ave., Detroit, MI _____
(Insert address)

AMOUNT OF GIFT (In figures): $__10,000.00____

AMOUNT OF GIFT (In words): $____Ten thousand_____ dollars

_____ *Henry Edsel Ford* _____
Your Signature

Full name and address of person or charity to receive cash gift.
(Name only one (1) person or charity here)
(Please print)_____ Harry J. Bennett III _____
(Insert name)

of _____ 3495 Lake Shore Drive, Grosse Pointe, Farms, MI _____
(Insert address)

AMOUNT OF GIFT (In figures): $__10,000.00____

AMOUNT OF GIFT (In words): $___Ten thousand_____ dollars

_____ *Henry Edsel Ford* _____
Your Signature

2.2     PERSONAL AND HOUSEHOLD ITEMS.

I may leave a separate list or statement either in my handwriting or signed by me at the end, regarding gifts of specific books, jewelry, clothing, automobiles, furniture, and other personal and household items.

I give my spouse all my books, jewelry, clothing, automobiles, furniture, and other personal and household items not included on any such separate list or statement.  If I am not married at the time I sign this will, or if my spouse dies before me, my personal representative shall distribute those items, as equally as possible, among my children who survive me.  If no children survive me, these items shall be distributed as set forth in paragraph 2.3.

Any inheritance tax due shall be paid from the balance of my estate and not from these gifts.

Page 2 of _7_ pages.

50

2.3    ALL OTHER ASSETS.

I give everything else I own to my spouse.  If I am not married at the time I sign this will, or if my spouse dies before me, I give these assets to my children and the descendants of any deceased child. If no spouse, children, or descendants of children survive me, I choose one of the following distribution clauses by signing my name on the line after that clause.  If I sign on both lines, or if I fail to sign on either line, or if I am not now married, these assets will go under distribution clause (b).

Distribution clause, if no spouse, children, or descendants of children survive me (Select only one).
(a)   One-half to be distributed to my heirs as if I did not have a will, and one-half to be distributed to my spouse's heirs as if my spouse had died just after me without a will.

<u>                    *Henry Edsel Ford*                    </u>
(Your Signature)

(b)   All to be distributed to my heirs as if I did not have a will.

<u>                                                         </u>
(Your Signature)

### ARTICLE 3. NOMINATIONS OF PERSONAL REPRESENTATIVE, GUARDIAN, AND CONSERVATOR

Personal representatives, guardians, and conservators have a great deal of responsibility.  The role of a personal representative is to collect your assets, pay debts and taxes from those assets, and distribute the remaining assets as directed in the will. A guardian is a person who will look after the physical well-being of a child.  A conservator is a person who will manage a child's assets and make payments from those assets for the child's benefit.  Select them carefully.  Also, before you select them, ask them whether they are willing and able to serve.

3.1    PERSONAL REPRESENTATIVE.  (Name at least one)

I nominate <u>        my wife, Holley Dodge Ford        </u>
(Insert name of person or eligible financial institution)

of <u>        8290 Lake Shore Drive, Grosse Point Farms, MI        </u>
(Insert address)
to serve as personal representative.

If my first choice does not serve, I nominate
<u>                my son, Joe Louis Ford                </u>
(Insert name of person or eligible financial institution)

of <u>        29642 Lone Pine Road, Orchard Lake, MI        </u>
(Insert address)
to serve as personal representative.

Page 3 of _7_ pages.

3.2    GUARDIAN AND CONSERVATOR.

Your spouse may die before you. Therefore, if you have a child under age 18, name a person as guardian of the child, and a person or eligible financial institution as conservator of the child's assets. The guardian and the conservator may, but need not be, the same person.

If a guardian or conservator is needed for any child of mine, I nominate

_____Allen Park, Jr._____
(Insert name or person)

of _____423 Orchard Lake Rd., Kego Harbor, MI_____ as guardian
(Insert address)

and _____Allen Park, Jr._____
(Insert name of person or eligible financial institution)

of _____423 Orchard Lake Rd., Kego Harbor, MI_____ as conservator.
(Insert address)

If my first choice cannot serve, I nominate

_____my daughter, Ann Allen Ford Fischer_____
(Insert name or person)

of _____1637 E. River Road, Grosse Ile, MI_____ as guardian
(Insert address)

and _____National Bank of Detroit_____
(Insert name of person or eligible financial institution)

of _____201 Jefferson Ave., Detroit, MI_____ as conservator.
(Insert address)

3.3    BOND.

A bond is a form of insurance in case your personal representative or a conservator performs improperly and jeopardizes your assets. A bond is not required. You may choose whether you wish to require your personal representative and any conservator to serve with or without bond. Bond premiums would be paid out of your assets.

(Select only one)

(a) My personal representative and any conservator I have named shall serve with bond.


_____
(Your Signature)


(b) My personal representative and any conservator I have named shall serve without bond.


_____*Henry Edsel Ford*_____
(Your Signature)

Page 4 of __7__ pages.

3.4    DEFINITIONS AND ADDITIONAL CLAUSES.

Definitions and additional clauses found at the end of this form are part of this will.

I sign my name to this Michigan statutory will on ___October 23_____, __1999___.

_____*Henry Edsel Ford*_____
(Your Signature)

## NOTICE REGARDING WITNESSES

You must use two (2) adult witnesses who will not receive assets under this will.  It is preferable to have three (3) adult witnesses.  All the witnesses must observe you sign the will, or have you tell them you signed the will, or have you tell them the will was signed at your direction in your presence.

## STATEMENT OF WITNESSES

We sign below as witnesses, declaring that the person who is making this will appears to be of sound mind and appears to be making this will freely and without duress, fraud, or undue influence and that the person making this will acknowledges that he or she has read, or has had it read to them, and understands the contents of this will.

Tom A. Edison
_____
(Print Name)
837 Pontiac Trail
_____
(Address)
Ann Arbor,     MI          48108
_____
(City)        (State)      (Zip)

*Tom A. Edison*
_____
(Signature of Witness)

Harvey Firestone IV
_____
(Print Name)
29305 Jolly Rd.
_____
(Address)
E. Lansing,    MI          48823
_____
(City)        (State)      (Zip)

*Harvey Firestone* IV
_____
(Signature of Witness)

## Definitions

The following definitions and rules of construction shall apply to this Michigan statutory will:

(a)   "Assets" means all types of property you can own, such as real estate, stocks and bonds, bank accounts, business interests, furniture, and automobiles.

(b)   "Jointly-held assets" means those assets ownership of which is transferred automatically upon death of 1 of the owners to the remaining owner or owners.

(c)   "Spouse" means your husband or wife at the time you sign this will.

(d)   "Descendants" means your children, grandchildren, and their descendants.

Page 5 of _7_ pages.

# Last Will and Testament

I, <u>John Smith</u> a resident of <u>Oakland</u> County, Michigan, declare this to be my will, hereby revoking any prior wills and codicils.

**FIRST:** I direct that all my debts and funeral expenses be paid out of my estate as soon after my death as is practicable.

**SECOND:** I may leave a separate statement or list disposing of certain items of my tangible personal property. Any such statement or list in existence at the time of my death shall be determinative with respect to all items bequeathed therein.

**THIRD:** I give, devise, and bequeath all my estate, real, personal, and mixed, of whatever kind and wherever situated, of which I may die seized or possessed, or in which I may have any interest or over which I may have any power of appointment or testamentary disposition, to my spouse, <u>Barbara Smith</u>. If my said spouse does not survive me, I give, and bequeath the said property to <u>my sisters, Jan Smith, Joan Smith, and Jennifer Smith Lee</u>, or the survivor of them.

**FOURTH:** In the event that any beneficiary fails to survive me by thirty days, then this will shall take effect as if that person had predeceased me.

**FIFTH:** I hereby nominate, constitute, and appoint <u>Barbara Smith</u> as Personal Representative of this, my Last Will and Testament. In the event that such named person is unable or unwilling to serve at any time or for any reason, then I nominate, constitute, and appoint <u>Reginald Smith</u> as Personal Representative in the place and stead of the person first named herein. It is my will and I direct that my Personal Representative shall not be required to furnish a bond for the faithful performance of his or her duties in any jurisdiction, any provision of law to the contrary notwithstanding, and I give my Personal Representative full power to administer my estate, including the power to settle claims, pay debts, and sell, lease or exchange real and personal property without court order.

IN WITNESS WHEREOF I have signed and published this Last Will and Testament, consisting of <u>2</u> page(s), this <u>23rd</u> day of <u>October</u>, <u>1999</u>.

John Smith

## STATEMENT OF WITNESSES

We sign below as witnesses, declaring that the person who is making this will appears to be of sound mind and appears to be making this will freely and without duress, fraud, or undue influence and that the person making this will acknowledges that he or she has read, or has had it read to them, and understands the contents of this will.

| *C. U. Sine* | *Justin Cayce* |
|---|---|
| (Signature of Witness) | (Signature of Witness) |
| C.U. Sine | Justin Cayce |
| (Print Name) | (Print Name) |
| 1428 N. Woodward Ave. | 243 Maple Rd. |
| (Address) | (Address) |
| Royal Oak,    MI    48073 | Birmingham,    MI    48009 |
| (City)    (State)    (Zip) | (City)    (State)    (Zip) |

# Last Will and Testament
# of

John Smith

I, <u>John Smith</u> a resident of <u>Kalamazoo</u> County, Michigan, declare this to be my will, hereby revoking any prior wills and codicils.

FIRST: I direct that all my debts and funeral expenses be paid out of my estate as soon after my death as is practicable.

SECOND: I may leave a separate statement or list disposing of certain items of my tangible personal property. Any such statement or list in existence at the time of my death shall be determinative with respect to all items bequeathed therein.

THIRD: I give, devise, and bequeath all my estate, real, personal, and mixed, of whatever kind and wherever situated, of which I may die seized or possessed, or in which I may have any interest or over which I may have any power of appointment or testamentary disposition, to my spouse, <u>Barbara Smith</u>. If my said spouse does not survive me, I give, and bequeath the said property to my children <u>Amy Smith, Beamy Smith, and, Seamy Smith</u>, in equal shares or to their lineal descendants, per stirpes.

FOURTH: In the event that any beneficiary fails to survive me by thirty days, then this will shall take effect as if that person had predeceased me.

FIFTH: I hereby nominate, constitute, and appoint <u>Barbara Smith</u> as Personal Representative of this, my Last Will and Testament. In the event that such named person is unable or unwilling to serve at any time or for any reason, then I nominate, constitute, and appoint <u>my brother, Reginald Smith</u> as Personal Representative in the place and stead of the person first named herein. It is my will and I direct that my Personal Representative shall not be required to furnish a bond for the faithful performance of his or her duties in any jurisdiction, any provision of law to the contrary notwithstanding, and I give my Personal Representative full power to administer my estate, including the power to settle claims, pay debts, and sell, lease or exchange real and personal property without court order.

Page 1 of 3 pages.

IN WITNESS WHEREOF I have signed and published this Last Will and Testament, consisting of two pages, this __5th__ day of __January__, __1999__ .

*John Smith*
_____

## STATEMENT OF WITNESSES

We sign below as witnesses, declaring that the person who is making this will appears to be of sound mind and appears to be making this will freely and without duress, fraud, or undue influence and that the person making this will acknowledges that he or she has read, or has had it read to them, and understands the contents of this will.

| C.U. Sine | *C.U. Sine* |
|---|---|
| (Print Name) | (Signature of Witness) |

1428 N. Woodward Ave.
_____
(Address)

| Royal Oak, | MI | 48073 |
|---|---|---|
| (City) | (State) | (Zip) |

| Justin Cayce | *Justin Cayce* |
|---|---|
| (Print Name) | (Signature of Witness) |

243 Maple Rd.
_____
(Address)

| Birmingham, | MI | 48009 |
|---|---|---|
| (City) | (State) | (Zip) |

Page 2 of _3_ pages.

# Last Will and Testament
# of

<u>John Doe</u>

I, _____John Doe_____ a resident of _____Kent_____ County, Michigan, declare this to be my will, hereby revoking any prior wills and codicils.

FIRST: I direct that all my debts and funeral expenses be paid out of my estate as soon after my death as is practicable.

SECOND: I may leave a separate statement or list disposing of certain items of my tangible personal property. Any such statement or list in existence at the time of my death shall be determinative with respect to all items bequeathed therein.

THIRD: I give, devise, and bequeath all my estate, real, personal, and mixed, of whatever kind and wherever situated, of which I may die seized or possessed, or in which I may have any interest or over which I may have any power of appointment or testamentary disposition, to my children _____James Doe, Mary Doe, Larry Doe, Barry Doe, Carrie Doe, and Moe Doe_____, plus any afterborn or adopted children in equal shares or to their lineal descendants per stirpes.

FOURTH: In the event that any beneficiary fails to survive me by thirty days, then this will shall take effect as if that person had predeceased me.

FIFTH: In the event any of my children have not attained the age of 18 years at the time of my death, I hereby nominate, constitute, and appoint <u>my brother, Herbert Doe</u> as guardian over the person of any of my children who have not reached the age of majority at the time of my death. In the event that said guardian is unable or unwilling to serve, then I nominate, constitute, and appoint <u>my brother Tom Doe</u> as guardian. Said guardian shall serve without bond or surety.

SIXTH: In the event any of my children have not attained the age of 18 years at the time of my death, I hereby nominate, constitute, and appoint <u>my brother Clarence Doe</u> as conservator over the property of any of my children who have not reached the age of majority at the time of my death. In the event that said conservator is unable or unwilling to serve, then I nominate, constitute, and appoint <u>my brother Englebert Doe</u> as conservator. Said conservator shall serve without bond or surety.

Page 1 of _3_ pages.

SEVENTH: I hereby nominate, constitute, and appoint <u>my brother, Clarence Doe</u> as Personal Representative of this, my Last Will and Testament. In the event that such named person is unable or unwilling to serve at any time or for any reason, then I nominate, constitute, and appoint <u>my brother, Englebert Doe</u> as Personal Representative in the place and stead of the person first named herein. It is my will and I direct that my Personal Representative shall not be required to furnish a bond for the faithful performance of his or her duties in any jurisdiction, any provision of law to the contrary notwithstanding, and I give my Personal Representative full power to administer my estate, including the power to settle claims, pay debts, and sell, lease or exchange real and personal property without court order.

IN WITNESS WHEREOF I have signed and published this Last Will and Testament, consisting of two pages, this __2nd__ day of _____July_____, __1999__.


*John Doe*
_____

## STATEMENT OF WITNESSES

We sign below as witnesses, declaring that the person who is making this will appears to be of sound mind and appears to be making this will freely and without duress, fraud, or undue influence and that the person making this will acknowledges that he or she has read, or has had it read to them, and understands the contents of this will.


C.U. Sine _____
               (Print Name)
5628 Alpine Ave. _____
               (Address)
Grand Rapids, MI       49512
 (City)       (State)     (Zip)

*C. U. Sine*
_____
       (Signature of Witness)


Justin Cayce _____
               (Print Name)
94 Grandville Ave. _____
               (Address)
Grand Rapids, MI       49546
 (City)       (State)     (Zip)

*Justin Cayce*
_____
       (Signature of Witness)

STATE OF MICHIGAN

COUNTY OF _____ Kent _____

    We, __John Doe_____, the testator, and __C.U. Sine_____, and __Justin Cayce_____, the witnesses, whose names are signed to the attached or foregoing instrument and whose signatures appear below, having been duly sworn, declared to the undersigned officer that: 1) the attached or foregoing instrument is the last will of the testator; 2) the testator willingly and voluntarily declared, signed, and executed the will in the presence of the witnesses; 3) the witnesses signed the will upon the request of the testator, in the presence and hearing of the testator and in the presence of each other; 4) to the best knowledge of each witness, the testator was, at the time of signing, of the age of majority (or otherwise legally competent to make a will), of sound mind and memory, and under no constraint, duress, fraud, or undue influence; 5) the testator acknowledged that he or she has read this will, or has had it read to him or her, and understands the contents of this will; and 6) each witness was and is competent and of proper age to witness a will.

_____*John Doe*_____ (Testator)

_____*C.U. Sine*_____ (Witness)

_____*Justin Cayce*_____ (Witness)

Subscribed and sworn to before me by _____John Doe_____, the testator, and by _____C.U. Sine_____ and _____Justin Cayce_____, the witnesses, all of whom personally appeared before me on __July 2_____, __1999___, each of whom is either personally known to me or produced identification as follows:

| Name: | Personally known/Identification |
|---|---|
| John Doe | Personally known |
| C.U. Sine | Mich. Dr. Lic. #S938774827 |
| Justin Cayce | Mich. Dr. Lic. #C987654321 |

_____

Mack A. Knau
Notary Public
My Commission Expires:

Page __3__ of __3__ pages.

# Codicil to the Will of

_____ Stirling Heitz _____

I, _____ Stirling Heitz _____, a resident of _____ Macomb _____
County, Michigan, declare this to be the first codicil to my Last Will and Testament dated
_____ January 5 _____, _____ 1993 _____.

FIRST: I hereby revoke the clause of my Will which reads as follows: _____
FOURTH: I hereby leave $5,000.00 to my daughter Mildred. _____

_____

_____.

SECOND: I hereby add the following clause to my Will: _____
FOURTH: I hereby leave $1,000.00 to my daughter Mildred. _____

_____

_____.

THIRD: In all other respects I hereby confirm and republish my Last Will and
Testament dated _____ January 5 _____, 1993 _____.

IN WITNESS WHEREOF, I have signed and published the foregoing instrument as
and for a codicil to my Last Will and Testament, this 23rd day of _____ August _____ 1999.

*Stirling Heitz*

_____

## STATEMENT OF WITNESSES

We sign below as witnesses, declaring that the person who is making this will appears to be of
sound mind and appears to be making this will freely and without duress, fraud, or undue influence
and that the person making this will acknowledges that he or she has read, or has had it read to them,
and understands the contents of this will.

| *Hazel Parke* | *Bob Lowe* |
|---|---|
| (Signature of Witness) | (Signature of Witness) |
| Hazel Parke | Bob Lowe |
| (Print Name) | (Print Name) |
| 192 Oakwood Blvd. | 819 Eureka Ave. |
| (Address) | (Address) |
| Dearborn,　　MI　　48124 | Southgate,　　MI　　48195 |
| (City)　　(State)　　(Zip) | (City)　　(State)　　(Zip) |

# Designation of Patient Advocate and Living Will

I, _____ Tiny Tim Cratchet _____, appoint _____ Bob Cratchet _____, whose address is 217 Christmas Past Circle, Bloomfield Hills, MI _____ and whose telephone number is __ (810) 555-5555 __, as my patient advocate pursuant to M.S.A. §27.5496; M.C.L.A. §700.496. I appoint _____ Mary Cratchet _____, whose address is 217 Christmas Past Circle, Bloomfield Hills, MI and whose telephone number is __ (810) 555-5555 __, as my alternate patient advocate in the event my patient advocate designated above does not accept the appointment, is incapacitated, or is removed. I authorize my patient advocate to make health care decisions for me when I am incapable of making my own heath care decisions, including decisions to withhold or withdraw medical treatment, even if such withholding or withdrawal could or would allow me to die. I understand the consequences of appointing a patient advocate.

I direct that my agent comply with the following instructions or limitations:
_____ none _____
_____.

I also direct that my patient advocate have authority to make decisions regarding the enforcement of my intentions regarding life-prolonging procedures as stated below:

I, _____ Tiny Tim Cratchet _____, being of sound mind willfully and voluntarily make known my desire that my dying shall not be artificially prolonged under the circumstances set forth below, do hereby declare:

If I should have an incurable or irreversible condition that will cause my death within a relatively short time, and if I am unable to make decisions regarding my medical treatment, I direct my attending physician to withhold or withdraw procedures that merely prolong the dying process and are not necessary to my comfort, or to alleviate pain.

This authorization [check only one box] ☐ includes ☒ does not include the withholding or withdrawal of artificial feeding and hydration.

Signed this __23rd__ day of __June__, __1999__.

*Tiny Tim Cratchet*
Signature
Address: 217 Christmas Past Circle
Bloomfield Hills, MI 48302

The declarant is personally known to me and voluntarily signed this document in my presence.

Witness: *Ebenezer Scrooge*     Witness: *Charles Dickens*
Name: Ebenezer Scrooge     Name: Charles Dickens
Address: 14285 Marley Ghost Dr.     Address: 452 Copperfield Ln.
Auburn Hills, MI 48321     Saugatuck, MI 49453

# Acceptance of Patient Advocate

I HEREBY accept the appointment as patient advocate and understand that:

(a) This designation shall not become effective unless the patient is unable to participate in medical decisions.

(b) A patient advocate shall not exercise powers concerning the patient's care, custody, and medical treatment that the patient, if the patient were able to participate in the decision, could not have exercised on his or her own behalf.

(c) This designation cannot be used to make a medical treatment decision to withhold or withdraw treatment from a patient who is pregnant that would result in the pregnant patient's death.

(d) A patient advocate may make a decision to withhold or withdraw treatment which would allow a patient to die only if the patient has expressed in a clear and convincing manner that the patient advocate is authorized to make such a decision, and that the patient acknowledges that such a decision could or would allow the patient's death.

(e) A patient advocate shall not receive compensation for the performance of his or her authority, rights, and responsibilities, but a patient advocate may be reimbursed for actual and necessary expenses incurred in the performance of his or her authority, rights, and responsibilities.

(f) A patient advocate shall act in accordance with the standards of care applicable to fiduciaries when acting for the patient and shall act consistent with the patient's best interests. The known desires of the patient expressed or evidenced while the patient is able to participate in medical treatment decisions are presumed to be in the patient's best interests.

(g) A patient may revoke his or her designation at any time and in any manner sufficient to communicate an intent to revoke.

(h) A patient advocate may revoke his or her acceptance to the designation at any time and in any manner sufficient to communicate an intent to revoke.

(i) A patient admitted to a health facility or agency has the rights enumerated in section 20201 of the public health code, Act No. 368 of the Public Acts of 1978, being section 33.20201 of the Michigan Compiled Laws.

Date: _June 23, 1999_____

_Bob Cratchet_____
Signature

# APPENDIX B
# FORMS

The following pages contain forms that can be used to prepare a will, codicil, designation of patient advocate and living will, and uniform donor card. They should only be used by persons who have read this book, who do not have any complications in their legal affairs, and who understand the forms they are using. The forms may be used right out of the book or they may be photocopied or retyped. It may be a good idea to use photocopies so you will have the originals in the book in case you make a mistake.

**Form 1. Asset and Beneficiary List.** *Use this form to keep an accurate record of your estate as well as your beneficiaries' names and addresses.*

**Form 2. Preferences and Information List.** *Use this form to let your family know of your wishes on matters not usually included in a will.*

**Form 3. Michigan Statutory Will.** *This is a will form provided in the Michigan statutes. Be sure to read the information on the Michigan Statutory Will on page 33 before you use this form.*

**Form 4. Simple Will**—Spouse and Minor Children—One Guardian/Conservator. *Use this will if you have minor children and want all your property to go to your spouse, but if your spouse dies previously, then to your minor children. It provides for one person to be guardian over your children and conservator over their estates.*

**Form 5. Simple Will**—Spouse and Minor Children—Separate Guardian and Conservator. *Use this will if you have minor children and want all your property to go to your spouse, but if your spouse dies previously, then to your minor children. It provides for two different people to serve as guardian over your children and conservator over their estates.*

**Form 6. Simple Will**—Spouse and Minor Children—Guardian and Trust. *Use this will if you have minor children and want all your property to go to your spouse, but if your spouse dies previously, then to your minor children. It provides for one person to be guardian over your children and for either the same person or another to be trustee over their property. The trust provision in this will allows your children's property to be held until they are older than eighteen, rather than distributing it all to them at age eighteen as would happen if you appointed a conservator.*

**Form 7. Simple Will**—Spouse and No Children. *Use this will if you want your property to go to your spouse, but if your spouse dies previously, to others or the* **survivor** *of the others.*

**Form 8. Simple Will**—Spouse and No Children. *Use this will if you want your property to go to your spouse, but if your spouse dies previously, to others or the* **descendants** *of the others.*

**Form 9. Simple Will**—Spouse and Adult Children. *Use this will if you want all of your property to go to your spouse, but if your spouse dies previously, then to your children, all of whom are adults.*

**Form 10. Simple Will**—Spouse and Adult Children. *Use this will if you want some of your property to go to your spouse, and some of your property to your children, all of whom are adults.*

**Form 11. Simple Will**—No Spouse—Minor Children—One Guardian/Conservator. *Use this will if you do not have a spouse and want all your property to go to your children, at least one of whom is a minor. It provides for one person to be guardian over your children and conservator over their estates.*

**Form 12. Simple Will**—No Spouse—Minor Children—Separate Guardian and Conservator. *Use this will if you do not have a spouse and want all your property to go to your children, at least one of whom is a minor. It provides for two different people to serve as guardian over your children and conservator over their estates.*

**Form 13. Simple Will**—No Spouse—Minor Children—Guardian and Trust. *Use this will if you do not have a spouse and want all your property to go to your children, at least one of whom is a minor. It provides for one person to be guardian over your children and for either that person or another to be trustee over their property. The trust provision in this will allows your children's property to be held until they are older than eighteen, rather than distributing it all to them at age eighteen as would happen if you appointed a conservator.*

**Form 14. Simple Will—No Spouse—Adult Children.** *This will should be used if you wish to leave your property to your adult children, or equally to each* **family** *if they predecease you.*

**Form 15. Simple Will—No Spouse—Adult Children.** *This will should be used if you wish to leave your property to your adult children, or equally to each* **person** *if they predecease you.*

**Form 16. Simple Will—No Spouse and No Children.** *Use this will if you have no spouse or children and want your property to go to the* **survivor** *of the people you name.*

**Form 17. Simple Will—No Spouse and No Children.** *Use this will if you have no spouse or children and want your property to go to the* **descendants** *of the people you name.*

**Form 18. Self-Proved Will Page.** *This page should be attached to every will as the last page. It must be witnessed and notarized.*

**Form 19. Codicil to Will.** *This form can be used to change one section of your will. Usually it is just as easy to execute a new will, since all of the same formalities are required.*

**Form 20. Self-Proved Codicil Page.** *If you decided to execute a codicil instead of making a new will, this page should be attached to your codicil as the last page. It must be witnessed and notarized.*

**Form 21. Designation of Patient Advocate and Living Will.** *This form is used to state that you do not want your life artificially prolonged if you have a terminal illness, and to designate a person to make medical decisions for you if you are unable to make such decisions yourself.*

**Form 22. Organ Donor Card.** *This form is used to spell out your wishes for donation of your body or any organs.*

# How to Pick the Right Will

If you do not use the Michigan Statutory Form (Form 3), you can follow this chart to find the right will for your situation. Then use Form 18 for the self-proved affidavit.

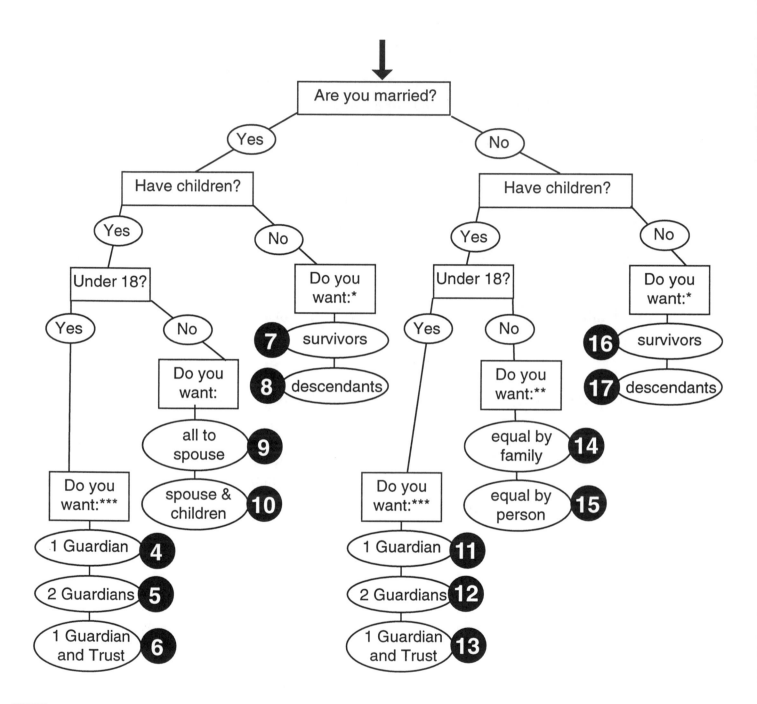

**18** Use the self-proving affidavit with all wills

\* For an explanation of survivors/decendants see page 27-28
\*\* For an explanation of families/persons see page 27-28
\*\*\* For an explanation of childrens' guardians and trust, see pages 29-30

# Asset and Beneficiary List

Property Inventory

**Assets**

Bank Accounts (checking, savings, certificates of deposit)

_____
_____
_____
_____
_____
_____
_____
_____

Real Estate

_____
_____
_____
_____
_____
_____
_____
_____

Vehicles (cars, trucks, boats, planes, RVs, etc.)

_____
_____
_____
_____
_____
_____
_____
_____

Personal Property (collections, jewelry, tools, artwork, household items, etc.)

_____
_____
_____
_____
_____
_____
_____

_____

_____

_____

_____

_____

_____

Stocks/Bonds/Mutual Funds

_____

_____

_____

_____

_____

_____

_____

_____

_____

_____

_____

Retirement Accounts (IRAs, 401(k)s, pension plans, etc.)

_____

_____

_____

_____

_____

_____

Receivables (mortgages held, notes, accounts receivable, personal loans)

_____

_____

_____

_____

_____

Life Insurance

_____

_____

_____

_____

_____

_____

_____

Other Property (trusts, partnerships, businesses, profit sharing, copyrights, etc.)

_____

_____

_____

_____

_____

_____

_____

## Liabilities

Real Estate Loans

_____

_____

_____

_____

_____

_____

_____

Vehicle Loans

_____

_____

_____

_____

_____

_____

_____

Other Secured Loans

_____
_____
_____
_____
_____
_____
_____

Unsecured Loans and Debts (taxes, child support, judgments, etc.)

_____
_____
_____
_____
_____
_____
_____
_____

**Beneficiary List**

Name_____  Address_____  Phone_____

_____
_____
_____
_____
_____
_____
_____
_____

# Preferences and Information List

## STATEMENT OF DESIRES AND LOCATION OF PROPERTY & DOCUMENTS

I, _____, am signing this document as the expression of my desires as to the matters stated below, and to inform my family members or other significant persons of the location of certain property and documents in the event of any emergency or of my death.

1.  **Funeral Desires.** It is my desire that the following arrangements be made for my funeral and disposition of remains in the event of my death (state if you have made any arrangements, such as pre-paid burial plans, cemetery plots owned, etc.):

    ❏   Burial at _____
    _____

    ❏   Cremation at _____
    _____

    ❏   Other specific desires: _____
    _____
    _____

2.  **Pets.** I have the following pet(s): _____
    _____. The following are my desires concerning the care of said pet(s): _____
    _____
    _____.

4.  **Notification.** I would like the following person(s) notified in the event of emergency or death (give name, address and phone number):
    _____
    _____
    _____
    _____
    _____.

5.  **Location of Documents.** The following is a list of important documents, and their location:

    ❏   Last Will and Testament, dated _____. Location: _____
    _____.

    ❏   Durable Power of Attorney, dated _____. Location: _____
    _____.

    ❏   Living Will, dated _____. Location: _____
    _____.

    ❏   Deed(s) to real estate (describe property location and location of deed):
    _____
    _____
    _____

❑ Title(s) to vehicles (cars, boats, etc.) (Describe vehicle, its location, and location of title, registration, or other documents):

_____
_____
_____
_____
_____

❑ Life insurance policies (list name address & phone number of insurance company and insurance agent, policy number, and location of policy):

_____
_____
_____
_____

❑ Other insurance policies (list type, company & agent, policy number, and location of policy):

_____
_____
_____
_____

❑ Other: (list other documents such as stock certificates, bonds, certificates of deposit, etc., and their location):

_____
_____
_____
_____

6.   **Location of Assets.** In addition to items readily visible in my home or listed above, I have the following assets:

❑ Safe deposit box located at _____

Box number _____ Key located at: _____

❑ Bank accounts (list name & address of bank, type of account, and account number):

_____
_____
_____
_____
_____
_____

❑ Other (describe the item and give its location):

_____
_____
_____
_____
_____
_____

7.   Other desires or information (state any desires or provide any information not given above; use additional sheets of paper if necessary):

_____
_____
_____
_____
_____
_____

Dated: _____        _____
                                     Signature

# MICHIGAN STATUTORY WILL
## NOTICE

1.  Any person age 18 or older and of sound mind may sign a will.
2.  There are several kinds of wills. If you choose to complete this form, you will have a Michigan statutory will. If this will does not meet your wishes in any way, you should talk with a lawyer before choosing a Michigan statutory will.
3.  Warning! It is strongly recommended that you do not add or cross out any words on this form except for filling in the blanks because all or part of this will may not be valid if you do so.
4.  This will has no effect on jointly-held assets, on retirement plan benefits, or on life insurance on your life if you have named a beneficiary who survives you.
5.  This will is not designed to reduce inheritance or estate taxes.
6.  This will treats adopted children and children born outside wedlock who would inherit if their parent died without a will the same way as children born or conceived during marriage.
7.  You should keep this will in your safe deposit box or other safe place. By paying a small fee, you may file the will in your county's probate court for safekeeping. You should tell your family where the will is kept.
8.  You may make and sign a new will at any time. If you marry or divorce after you sign this will, you should make a new will.

INSTRUCTIONS:

1.  To have a Michigan statutory will, you must complete the blanks on the will form. You may do this yourself, or direct someone to do it for you. You must either sign the will or direct someone else to sign it in your name and in your presence.
2.  Read the entire Michigan statutory will carefully before you begin filling in the blanks. If there is anything you do not understand, you should ask a lawyer to explain it to you.

## MICHIGAN STATUTORY WILL OF

_____

(Print or type your full name)

### ARTICLE 1. DECLARATIONS

This is my will and I revoke any prior wills and codicils. I live in _____ County, Michigan.

My spouse is _____

(Insert spouse's name or write "None")

My children now living are:

_____          _____

(Insert names or write "None")

_____          _____

_____          _____

Page 1 of ___ pages.

## ARTICLE 2. DISPOSITION OF MY ASSETS

2.1    CASH GIFTS TO PERSONS OR CHARITIES. (Optional)

I can leave no more that two (2) cash gifts. I make the following cash gifts to the persons or charities in the amounts stated here. Any inheritance tax due shall be paid from the balance of my estate and not from these gifts.

Full name and address of person or charity to receive cash gift.
(Name only one (1) person or charity here)
(Please print)_____
(Insert name)

of _____
(Insert address)

AMOUNT OF GIFT (In figures): $_____

AMOUNT OF GIFT (In words): $_____ dollars


_____
Your Signature

Full name and address of person or charity to receive cash gift.
(Name only one (1) person or charity here)
(Please print)_____
(Insert name)

of _____
(Insert address)

AMOUNT OF GIFT (In figures): $_____

AMOUNT OF GIFT (In words): $_____ dollars


_____
Your Signature

2.2    PERSONAL AND HOUSEHOLD ITEMS.

I may leave a separate list or statement either in my handwriting or signed by me at the end, regarding gifts of specific books, jewelry, clothing, automobiles, furniture, and other personal and household items.

I give my spouse all my books, jewelry, clothing, automobiles, furniture, and other personal and household items not included on any such separate list or statement. If I am not married at the time I sign this will, or if my spouse dies before me, my personal representative shall distribute those items, as equally as possible, among my children who survive me. If no children survive me, these items shall be distributed as set forth in paragraph 2.3.

Any inheritance tax due shall be paid from the balance of my estate and not from these gifts.

Page 2 of ___ pages.

## 2.3    ALL OTHER ASSETS.

I give everything else I own to my spouse. If I am not married at the time I sign this will, or if my spouse dies before me, I give these assets to my children and the descendants of any deceased child. If no spouse, children, or descendants of children survive me, I choose one of the following distribution clauses by signing my name on the line after that clause. If I sign on both lines, or if I fail to sign on either line, or if I am not now married, these assets will go under distribution clause (b).

Distribution clause, if no spouse, children, or descendants of children survive me (Select only one).
(a)   One-half to be distributed to my heirs as if I did not have a will, and one-half to be distributed to my spouse's heirs as if my spouse had died just after me without a will.

_____

(Your Signature)

(b)   All to be distributed to my heirs as if I did not have a will.

_____

(Your Signature)

## ARTICLE 3. NOMINATIONS OF PERSONAL REPRESENTATIVE, GUARDIAN, AND CONSERVATOR

Personal representatives, guardians, and conservators have a great deal of responsibility. The role of a personal representative is to collect your assets, pay debts and taxes from those assets, and distribute the remaining assets as directed in the will. A guardian is a person who will look after the physical well-being of a child. A conservator is a person who will manage a child's assets and make payments from those assets for the child's benefit. Select them carefully. Also, before you select them, ask them whether they are willing and able to serve.

## 3.1    PERSONAL REPRESENTATIVE. (Name at least one)

I nominate _____
(Insert name of person or eligible financial institution)

of _____
(Insert address)
to serve as personal representative.

If my first choice does not serve, I nominate

_____
(Insert name of person or eligible financial institution)

of _____
(Insert address)
to serve as personal representative.

## 3.2 GUARDIAN AND CONSERVATOR.

Your spouse may die before you. Therefore, if you have a child under age 18, name a person as guardian of the child, and a person or eligible financial institution as conservator of the child's assets. The guardian and the conservator may, but need not be, the same person.

If a guardian or conservator is needed for any child of mine, I nominate

_____

(Insert name or person)

of _____ as guardian

(Insert address)

and _____

(Insert name of person or eligible financial institution)

of _____ as conservator.

(Insert address)

If my first choice cannot serve, I nominate

_____

(Insert name or person)

of _____ as guardian

(Insert address)

and _____

(Insert name of person or eligible financial institution)

of _____ as conservator.

(Insert address)

## 3.3 BOND.

A bond is a form of insurance in case your personal representative or a conservator performs improperly and jeopardizes your assets. A bond is not required. You may choose whether you wish to require your personal representative and any conservator to serve with or without bond. Bond premiums would be paid out of your assets.

(Select only one)

(a) My personal representative and any conservator I have named shall serve with bond.

_____

(Your Signature)

(b) My personal representative and any conservator I have named shall serve without bond.

_____

(Your Signature)

Page 4 of ____ pages.

## 3.4  DEFINITIONS AND ADDITIONAL CLAUSES.

Definitions and additional clauses found at the end of this form are part of this will.

I sign my name to this Michigan statutory will on _____, _____.

_____
(Your Signature)

### NOTICE REGARDING WITNESSES

You must use two (2) adult witnesses who will not receive assets under this will. It is preferable to have three (3) adult witnesses. All the witnesses must observe you sign the will, or have you tell them you signed the will, or have you tell them the will was signed at your direction in your presence.

### STATEMENT OF WITNESSES

We sign below as witnesses, declaring that the person who is making this will appears to be of sound mind and appears to be making this will freely and without duress, fraud, or undue influence and that the person making this will acknowledges that he or she has read, or has had it read to them, and understands the contents of this will.

_____        _____
(Print Name)                          (Signature of Witness)

_____
(Address)

_____
(City)        (State)        (Zip)

_____        _____
(Print Name)                          (Signature of Witness)

_____
(Address)

_____
(City)        (State)        (Zip)

### Definitions

The following definitions and rules of construction shall apply to this Michigan statutory will:

(a)  "Assets" means all types of property you can own, such as real estate, stocks and bonds, bank accounts, business interests, furniture, and automobiles.

(b)  "Jointly-held assets" means those assets ownership of which is transferred automatically upon death of 1 of the owners to the remaining owner or owners.

(c)  "Spouse" means your husband or wife at the time you sign this will.

(d)  "Descendants" means your children, grandchildren, and their descendants.

Page 5 of \_\_\_ pages.

(e) "Descendants" or "children" includes persons born or conceived during marriage, persons legally adopted, and persons born out of wedlock who would inherit if their parent died without a will.

(f) Whenever a distribution under a Michigan statutory will is to be made to a person's descendants, the assets are to be divided into as many equal shares as there are then living descendants of the nearest degree of living descendants and deceased descendants of that same degree who leave living descendants. Each living descendant of the nearest degree shall receive 1 share. The share of each deceased descendant of that same degree shall be divided among his or her descendants in the same manner.

(g) "Heirs" means those persons who would have received your assets if you had died without a will, domiciled in Michigan, under the laws which are then in effect.

(h) "Person" includes individuals and institutions.

(i) Plural and singular words include each other, where appropriate.

(j) If a Michigan statutory will states that a person shall perform an act, the person is required to perform that act. If a Michigan statutory will states that a person may do an act, the person's decision to do or not do the act shall be made in a good faith exercise of the person's powers.

## Additional Clauses

(a) Powers of personal representative.

(1) The personal representative shall have all powers of administration given by Michigan law to independent personal representatives, and the power to invest and reinvest the estate from time to time in any property, real or personal, even though such investment, by reason of its character, amount, proportion to the total estate, or otherwise, would not be considered appropriate for a fiduciary apart from this provision. In dividing and distributing the estate, the personal representative may distribute partially or totally in kind, may determine the value of distributions in kind without reference to income tax basis, and may make non pro rata distributions.

(2) The personal representative may distribute estate assets otherwise distributable to a minor beneficiary to (a) the conservator, or (b) in amounts not exceeding $5,000.00 per year, either to the minor, if married; to a parent or any adult person with whom the minor resides and who has the care, custody, or control of the minor; or the guardian. The personal representative is free of liability and is discharged from any further accountability for distributing assets in compliance with the provisions of this paragraph.

(b) Powers of guardian and conservator. A guardian named in this will shall have the same authority with respect to the child as a parent having legal custody would have. A conservator named in this will shall have all of the powers conferred by law.

Page 6 of ___ pages.

# Last Will and Testament
# of

_____

I, _____ a resident of _____ County, Michigan, declare this to be my will, hereby revoking any prior wills and codicils.

FIRST: I direct that all my debts and funeral expenses be paid out of my estate as soon after my death as is practicable.

SECOND: I may leave a separate statement or list disposing of certain items of my tangible personal property. Any such statement or list in existence at the time of my death shall be determinative with respect to all items bequeathed therein.

THIRD: I give, devise, and bequeath all my estate, real, personal, and mixed, of whatever kind and wherever situated, of which I may die seized or possessed, or in which I may have any interest or over which I may have any power of appointment or testamentary disposition, to my spouse, _____. If my said spouse does not survive me, I give, and bequeath the said property to my children _____ _____ _____, plus any afterborn or adopted children in equal shares or their lineal descendants, per stirpes.

FOURTH: In the event that any beneficiary fails to survive me by thirty days, then this will shall take effect as if that person had predeceased me.

FIFTH: Should my spouse not survive me, I hereby nominate, constitute, and appoint _____ as guardian over the person and as conservator over the estate of any of my children who have not reached the age of majority at the time of my death. In the event that said guardian/conservator is unable or unwilling to serve, then I nominate, constitute, and appoint _____ as guardian/conservator. Said guardian shall serve without bond or surety.

SIXTH: I hereby nominate, constitute, and appoint _____ as Personal Representative of this, my Last Will and Testament. In the event that such named person is unable or unwilling to serve at any time or for any reason, then I nominate, constitute, and appoint _____ as Personal Representative in the place and stead of the person first named herein. It is my will and I direct that my Personal Representative shall not be required to furnish a bond for the faithful performance of his or

Page 1 of ___ pages.

her duties in any jurisdiction, any provision of law to the contrary notwithstanding, and I give my Personal Representative full power to administer my estate, including the power to settle claims, pay debts, and sell, lease or exchange real and personal property without court order.

IN WITNESS WHEREOF I have signed and published this Last Will and Testament, consisting of two pages, this _____ day of _____, _____.

_____

## STATEMENT OF WITNESSES

We sign below as witnesses, declaring that the person who is making this will appears to be of sound mind and appears to be making this will freely and without duress, fraud, or undue influence and that the person making this will acknowledges that he or she has read, or has had it read to them, and understands the contents of this will.

| | |
|---|---|
| _____ | _____ |
| (Print Name) | (Signature of Witness) |
| _____ | |
| (Address) | |
| _____ | |
| (City)        (State)        (Zip) | |

| | |
|---|---|
| _____ | _____ |
| (Print Name) | (Signature of Witness) |
| _____ | |
| (Address) | |
| _____ | |
| (City)        (State)        (Zip) | |

Page 2 of ____ pages.

# Last Will and Testament
# of

_____

I, _____ a resident of _____ County, Michigan, declare this to be my will, hereby revoking any prior wills and codicils.

FIRST: I direct that all my debts and funeral expenses be paid out of my estate as soon after my death as is practicable.

SECOND: I may leave a separate statement or list disposing of certain items of my tangible personal property. Any such statement or list in existence at the time of my death shall be determinative with respect to all items bequeathed therein.

THIRD: I give, devise, and bequeath all my estate, real, personal, and mixed, of whatever kind and wherever situated, of which I may die seized or possessed, or in which I may have any interest or over which I may have any power of appointment or testamentary disposition, to my spouse, _____. If my said spouse does not survive me, I give, and bequeath the said property to my children _____ _____ _____, plus any afterborn or adopted children in equal shares or their lineal descendants, per stirpes.

FOURTH: In the event that any beneficiary fails to survive me by thirty days, then this will shall take effect as if that person had predeceased me.

FIFTH: Should my spouse not survive me, I hereby nominate, constitute, and appoint _____, as guardian over the person of any of my children who have not reached the age of majority at the time of my death. In the event that said guardian is unable or unwilling to serve, then I nominate, constitute, and appoint _____ as guardian. Said guardian shall serve without bond or surety.

SIXTH: Should my spouse not survive me, I hereby nominate, constitute, and appoint _____ as conservator over the estate of any of my children who have not reached the age of majority at the time of my death. In the event that said conservator is unable or unwilling to serve, then I nominate, constitute, and appoint _____ as conservator. Said conservator shall serve without bond or surety.

Page 1 of ____ pages.

SEVENTH: I hereby nominate, constitute, and appoint _____ as Personal Representative of this, my Last Will and Testament. In the event that such named person is unable or unwilling to serve at any time or for any reason, then I nominate, constitute, and appoint _____ as Personal Representative in the place and stead of the person first named herein. It is my will and I direct that my Personal Representative shall not be required to furnish a bond for the faithful performance of his or her duties in any jurisdiction, any provision of law to the contrary notwithstanding, and I give my Personal Representative full power to administer my estate, including the power to settle claims, pay debts, and sell, lease or exchange real and personal property without court order.

IN WITNESS WHEREOF I have signed and published this Last Will and Testament, consisting of two pages, this _____ day of _____, _____.

_____

## STATEMENT OF WITNESSES

We sign below as witnesses, declaring that the person who is making this will appears to be of sound mind and appears to be making this will freely and without duress, fraud, or undue influence and that the person making this will acknowledges that he or she has read, or has had it read to them, and understands the contents of this will.

| _____ | _____ |
| (Print Name) | (Signature of Witness) |
| _____ | |
| (Address) | |

| (City) | (State) | (Zip) |

| _____ | _____ |
| (Print Name) | (Signature of Witness) |
| _____ | |
| (Address) | |

| (City) | (State) | (Zip) |

# Last Will and Testament
# of

_____

I, _____ a resident of _____ County, Michigan, declare this to be my will, hereby revoking any prior wills and codicils.

FIRST: I direct that all my debts and funeral expenses be paid out of my estate as soon after my death as is practicable.

SECOND: I may leave a separate statement or list disposing of certain items of my tangible personal property. Any such statement or list in existence at the time of my death shall be determinative with respect to all items bequeathed therein.

THIRD: I give, devise, and bequeath all my estate, real, personal, and mixed, of whatever kind and wherever situated, of which I may die seized or possessed, or in which I may have any interest or over which I may have any power of appointment or testamentary disposition, to my spouse, _____. If my said spouse does not survive me, I give, and bequeath the said property to my children _____ _____ _____, plus any afterborn or adopted children in equal shares or their lineal descendants, per stirpes.

FOURTH: In the event that any beneficiary fails to survive me by thirty days, then this will shall take effect as if that person had predeceased me.

FIFTH: In the event that any of my children have not reached the age of _____ years at the time of my death, then the share of any such child shall be held in a separate trust by _____ for such child.

The trustee shall use the income and that part of the principal of the trust as is, in the trustee's sole discretion, necessary or desirable to provide proper housing, medical care, food, clothing, entertainment and education for the trust beneficiary, considering the beneficiary's other resources. Any income that is not distributed shall be added to the principal. Additionally, the trustee shall have all powers conferred by the law of the state having jurisdiction over this trust, as well as the power to pay from the assets of the trust reasonable fees necessary to administer the trust.

The trust shall terminate when the child reaches the age specified above and the remaining assets distributed to the child, unless they have been exhausted sooner. In the event the child dies prior to the termination of the trust, then the assets shall pass to the estate of the child. The interests of the beneficiary under this trust shall not be assignable and shall be free from the claims of creditors to the full extent allowed by law.

Page 1 of ___ pages.

In the event the said trustee is unable or unwilling to serve for any reason, then I nominate, constitute, and appoint _____ as alternate trustee. No bond shall be required of either trustee in any jurisdiction and this trust shall be administered without court supervision as allowed by law.

SIXTH: Should my spouse not survive me, I hereby nominate, constitute, and appoint _____ as guardian over the person of any of my children who have not reached the age of majority at the time of my death. In the event that said guardian is unable or unwilling to serve, then I nominate, constitute, and appoint _____ _____ as guardian.

SEVENTH: I hereby nominate, constitute, and appoint _____ as Personal Representative of this, my Last Will and Testament. In the event that such named person is unable or unwilling to serve at any time or for any reason, then I nominate, constitute, and appoint _____ as Personal Representative in the place and stead of the person first named herein. It is my will and I direct that my Personal Representative shall not be required to furnish a bond for the faithful performance of his or her duties in any jurisdiction, any provision of law to the contrary notwithstanding, and I give my Personal Representative full power to administer my estate, including the power to settle claims, pay debts, and sell, lease or exchange real and personal property without court order.

IN WITNESS WHEREOF I have signed and published this Last Will and Testament, consisting of two pages, this _____ day of _____, _____.

_____

STATEMENT OF WITNESSES

We sign below as witnesses, declaring that the person who is making this will appears to be of sound mind and appears to be making this will freely and without duress, fraud, or undue influence and that the person making this will acknowledges that he or she has read, or has had it read to them, and understands the contents of this will.

_____          _____
(Signature of Witness)                                  (Signature of Witness)

_____          _____
(Print Name)                                              (Print Name)

_____          _____
(Address)                                                 (Address)

_____          _____
(City)          (State)          (Zip)                  (City)          (State)          (Zip)

# Last Will and Testament

I, _____ a resident of _____
County, Michigan, declare this to be my will, hereby revoking any prior wills and codicils.

**FIRST:** I direct that all my debts and funeral expenses be paid out of my estate as soon after my death as is practicable.

**SECOND:** I may leave a separate statement or list disposing of certain items of my tangible personal property. Any such statement or list in existence at the time of my death shall be determinative with respect to all items bequeathed therein.

**THIRD:** I give, devise, and bequeath all my estate, real, personal, and mixed, of whatever kind and wherever situated, of which I may die seized or possessed, or in which I may have any interest or over which I may have any power of appointment or testamentary disposition, to my spouse, _____. If my said spouse does not survive me, I give, and bequeath the said property to _____ _____, or the survivor of them.

**FOURTH:** In the event that any beneficiary fails to survive me by thirty days, then this will shall take effect as if that person had predeceased me.

**FIFTH:** I hereby nominate, constitute, and appoint _____ as Personal Representative of this, my Last Will and Testament. In the event that such named person is unable or unwilling to serve at any time or for any reason, then I nominate, constitute, and appoint _____ as Personal Representative in the place and stead of the person first named herein. It is my will and I direct that my Personal Representative shall not be required to furnish a bond for the faithful performance of his or her duties in any jurisdiction, any provision of law to the contrary notwithstanding, and I give my Personal Representative full power to administer my estate, including the power to settle claims, pay debts, and sell, lease or exchange real and personal property without court order.

IN WITNESS WHEREOF I have signed and published this Last Will and Testament, consisting of two pages, this _____ day of _____, _____.

_____

## STATEMENT OF WITNESSES

We sign below as witnesses, declaring that the person who is making this will appears to be of sound mind and appears to be making this will freely and without duress, fraud, or undue influence and that the person making this will acknowledges that he or she has read, or has had it read to them, and understands the contents of this will.

| _____ | _____ |
| (Signature of Witness) | (Signature of Witness) |
| _____ | _____ |
| (Print Name) | (Print Name) |
| _____ | _____ |
| (Address) | (Address) |

| _____ | _____ | _____ | _____ | _____ | _____ |
| (City) | (State) | (Zip) | (City) | (State) | (Zip) |

# Last Will and Testament
## of

_____

I, _____ a resident of _____ County, Michigan, declare this to be my will, hereby revoking any prior wills and codicils.

FIRST: I direct that all my debts and funeral expenses be paid out of my estate as soon after my death as is practicable.

SECOND: I may leave a separate statement or list disposing of certain items of my tangible personal property. Any such statement or list in existence at the time of my death shall be determinative with respect to all items bequeathed therein.

THIRD: I give, devise, and bequeath all my estate, real, personal, and mixed, of whatever kind and wherever situated, of which I may die seized or possessed, or in which I may have any interest or over which I may have any power of appointment or testamentary disposition, to my spouse, _____. If my said spouse does not survive me, I give, and bequeath the said property to _____

_____

_____

_____,

or to their lineal descendants, per stirpes.

FOURTH: In the event that any beneficiary fails to survive me by thirty days, then this will shall take effect as if that person had predeceased me.

FIFTH: I hereby nominate, constitute, and appoint _____ as Personal Representative of this, my Last Will and Testament. In the event that such named person is unable or unwilling to serve at any time or for any reason, then I nominate, constitute, and appoint _____ as Personal Representative in the place and stead of the person first named herein. It is my will and I direct that my Personal Representative shall not be required to furnish a bond for the faithful performance of his or her duties in any jurisdiction, any provision of law to the contrary notwithstanding, and I give my Personal Representative full power to administer my estate, including the power to settle claims, pay debts, and sell, lease or exchange real and personal property without court order.

Page 1 of ___ pages.

IN WITNESS WHEREOF I have signed and published this Last Will and Testament, consisting of two pages, this _____ day of _____, _____.

_____

## STATEMENT OF WITNESSES

We sign below as witnesses, declaring that the person who is making this will appears to be of sound mind and appears to be making this will freely and without duress, fraud, or undue influence and that the person making this will acknowledges that he or she has read, or has had it read to them, and understands the contents of this will.

_____
(Print Name)

_____
(Signature of Witness)

_____
(Address)

_____
(City)          (State)          (Zip)

_____
(Print Name)

_____
(Signature of Witness)

_____
(Address)

_____
(City)          (State)          (Zip)

Page 2 of ___ pages.

# Last Will and Testament
## of

_____

I, _____ a resident of _____ County, Michigan, declare this to be my will, hereby revoking any prior wills and codicils.

FIRST: I direct that all my debts and funeral expenses be paid out of my estate as soon after my death as is practicable.

SECOND: I may leave a separate statement or list disposing of certain items of my tangible personal property. Any such statement or list in existence at the time of my death shall be determinative with respect to all items bequeathed therein.

THIRD: I give, devise, and bequeath all my estate, real, personal, and mixed, of whatever kind and wherever situated, of which I may die seized or possessed, or in which I may have any interest or over which I may have any power of appointment or testamentary disposition, to my spouse, _____. If my said spouse does not survive me, I give, and bequeath the said property to my children _____

_____

_____

_____,

in equal shares or to their lineal descendants, per stirpes.

FOURTH: In the event that any beneficiary fails to survive me by thirty days, then this will shall take effect as if that person had predeceased me.

FIFTH: I hereby nominate, constitute, and appoint _____ as Personal Representative of this, my Last Will and Testament. In the event that such named person is unable or unwilling to serve at any time or for any reason, then I nominate, constitute, and appoint _____ as Personal Representative in the place and stead of the person first named herein. It is my will and I direct that my Personal Representative shall not be required to furnish a bond for the faithful performance of his or her duties in any jurisdiction, any provision of law to the contrary notwithstanding, and I give my Personal Representative full power to administer my estate, including the power to settle claims, pay debts, and sell, lease or exchange real and personal property without court order.

Page 1 of ___ pages.

IN WITNESS WHEREOF I have signed and published this Last Will and Testament, consisting of two pages, this _____ day of _____, _____.


_____


## STATEMENT OF WITNESSES

We sign below as witnesses, declaring that the person who is making this will appears to be of sound mind and appears to be making this will freely and without duress, fraud, or undue influence and that the person making this will acknowledges that he or she has read, or has had it read to them, and understands the contents of this will.


_____          _____
(Print Name)                                    (Signature of Witness)

_____
(Address)

_____
(City)        (State)        (Zip)


_____          _____
(Print Name)                                    (Signature of Witness)

_____
(Address)

_____
(City)        (State)        (Zip)


Page 2 of ___ pages.

# Last Will and Testament
# of

_____

I, _____ a resident of _____ County, Michigan, declare this to be my will, hereby revoking any prior wills and codicils.

FIRST: I direct that all my debts and funeral expenses be paid out of my estate as soon after my death as is practicable.

SECOND: I may leave a separate statement or list disposing of certain items of my tangible personal property. Any such statement or list in existence at the time of my death shall be determinative with respect to all items bequeathed therein.

THIRD: I give, devise, and bequeath all my estate, real, personal, and mixed, of whatever kind and wherever situated, of which I may die seized or possessed, or in which I may have any interest or over which I may have any power of appointment or testamentary disposition, as follows:

_____% to my spouse, _____ and

_____% to my children, _____

_____

_____,

in equal shares or to their lineal descendants per stirpes.

FOURTH: In the event that any beneficiary fails to survive me by thirty days, then this will shall take effect as if that person had predeceased me.

FIFTH: I hereby nominate, constitute, and appoint _____ as Personal Representative of this, my Last Will and Testament. In the event that such named person is unable or unwilling to serve at any time or for any reason, then I nominate, constitute, and appoint _____ as Personal Representative in the place and stead of the person first named herein. It is my will and I direct that my Personal Representative shall not be required to furnish a bond for the faithful performance of his or her duties in any jurisdiction, any provision of law to the contrary notwithstanding, and I give my Personal Representative full power to administer my estate, including the power to settle claims, pay debts, and sell, lease or exchange real and personal property without court order.

Page 1 of \_\_\_ pages.

IN WITNESS WHEREOF I have signed and published this Last Will and Testament, consisting of two pages, this _____ day of _____, _____.


_____


## STATEMENT OF WITNESSES

We sign below as witnesses, declaring that the person who is making this will appears to be of sound mind and appears to be making this will freely and without duress, fraud, or undue influence and that the person making this will acknowledges that he or she has read, or has had it read to them, and understands the contents of this will.

_____        _____
(Print Name)                                (Signature of Witness)

_____
(Address)

_____
(City)        (State)        (Zip)


_____        _____
(Print Name)                                (Signature of Witness)

_____
(Address)

_____
(City)        (State)        (Zip)


Page 2 of ___ pages.

# Last Will and Testament
# of

_____

I, _____ a resident of _____ County, Michigan, declare this to be my will, hereby revoking any prior wills and codicils.

FIRST: I direct that all my debts and funeral expenses be paid out of my estate as soon after my death as is practicable.

SECOND: I may leave a separate statement or list disposing of certain items of my tangible personal property. Any such statement or list in existence at the time of my death shall be determinative with respect to all items bequeathed therein.

THIRD: I give, devise, and bequeath all my estate, real, personal, and mixed, of whatever kind and wherever situated, of which I may die seized or possessed, or in which I may have any interest or over which I may have any power of appointment or testamentary disposition, to my children _____

_____

_____,
plus any afterborn or adopted children in equal shares or to their lineal descendants per stirpes.

FOURTH: In the event that any beneficiary fails to survive me by thirty days, then this will shall take effect as if that person had predeceased me.

FIFTH: In the event any of my children have not attained the age of 18 years at the time of my death, I hereby nominate, constitute, and appoint _____ as guardian over the person and conservator over the estate of any of my children who have not reached the age of majority at the time of my death. In the event that said guardian/conservator is unable or unwilling to serve, then I nominate, constitute, and appoint _____ as guardian/conservator. Said guardian/conservator shall serve without bond or surety.

SIXTH: I hereby nominate, constitute, and appoint _____ as Personal Representative of this, my Last Will and Testament. In the event that such named person is unable or unwilling to serve at any time or for any reason, then I nominate, constitute, and appoint _____ as Personal Representative in the place and stead of the person first named herein. It is my will and I direct that my Personal

Page 1 of ___ pages.

Representative shall not be required to furnish a bond for the faithful performance of his or her duties in any jurisdiction, any provision of law to the contrary notwithstanding, and I give my Personal Representative full power to administer my estate, including the power to settle claims, pay debts, and sell, lease or exchange real and personal property without court order.

IN WITNESS WHEREOF I have signed and published this Last Will and Testament, consisting of two pages, this _____ day of _____, _____.

_____

### STATEMENT OF WITNESSES

We sign below as witnesses, declaring that the person who is making this will appears to be of sound mind and appears to be making this will freely and without duress, fraud, or undue influence and that the person making this will acknowledges that he or she has read, or has had it read to them, and understands the contents of this will.

_____          _____
            (Print Name)                              (Signature of Witness)
_____
            (Address)
_____
(City)      (State)      (Zip)


_____          _____
            (Print Name)                              (Signature of Witness)
_____
            (Address)
_____
(City)      (State)      (Zip)

# Last Will and Testament
# of

_____

I, _____ a resident of _____
County, Michigan, declare this to be my will, hereby revoking any prior wills and codicils.

FIRST: I direct that all my debts and funeral expenses be paid out of my estate as soon after my death as is practicable.

SECOND: I may leave a separate statement or list disposing of certain items of my tangible personal property. Any such statement or list in existence at the time of my death shall be determinative with respect to all items bequeathed therein.

THIRD: I give, devise, and bequeath all my estate, real, personal, and mixed, of whatever kind and wherever situated, of which I may die seized or possessed, or in which I may have any interest or over which I may have any power of appointment or testamentary disposition, to my children _____
_____
_____,
plus any afterborn or adopted children in equal shares or to their lineal descendants per stirpes.

FOURTH: In the event that any beneficiary fails to survive me by thirty days, then this will shall take effect as if that person had predeceased me.

FIFTH: In the event any of my children have not attained the age of 18 years at the time of my death, I hereby nominate, constitute, and appoint _____
as guardian over the person of any of my children who have not reached the age of majority at the time of my death. In the event that said guardian is unable or unwilling to serve, then I nominate, constitute, and appoint _____ as guardian. Said guardian shall serve without bond or surety.

SIXTH: In the event any of my children have not attained the age of 18 years at the time of my death, I hereby nominate, constitute, and appoint _____
as conservator over the property of any of my children who have not reached the age of majority at the time of my death. In the event that said conservator is unable or unwilling to serve, then I nominate, constitute, and appoint _____
as conservator. Said conservator shall serve without bond or surety.

Page 1 of ___ pages.

SEVENTH: I hereby nominate, constitute, and appoint _____ as Personal Representative of this, my Last Will and Testament. In the event that such named person is unable or unwilling to serve at any time or for any reason, then I nominate, constitute, and appoint _____ as Personal Representative in the place and stead of the person first named herein. It is my will and I direct that my Personal Representative shall not be required to furnish a bond for the faithful performance of his or her duties in any jurisdiction, any provision of law to the contrary notwithstanding, and I give my Personal Representative full power to administer my estate, including the power to settle claims, pay debts, and sell, lease or exchange real and personal property without court order.

IN WITNESS WHEREOF I have signed and published this Last Will and Testament, consisting of two pages, this _____ day of _____, _____.


_____


## STATEMENT OF WITNESSES

We sign below as witnesses, declaring that the person who is making this will appears to be of sound mind and appears to be making this will freely and without duress, fraud, or undue influence and that the person making this will acknowledges that he or she has read, or has had it read to them, and understands the contents of this will.


| _____ | _____ |
| (Print Name) | (Signature of Witness) |

_____
(Address)

_____
(City)  (State)  (Zip)


| _____ | _____ |
| (Print Name) | (Signature of Witness) |

_____
(Address)

_____
(City)  (State)  (Zip)

Page 2 of ___ pages.

# Last Will and Testament

I, _____ a resident of _____
County, Michigan, declare this to be my will, hereby revoking any prior wills and codicils.

FIRST: I direct that all my debts and funeral expenses be paid out of my estate as soon after my death as is practicable.

SECOND: I may leave a separate statement or list disposing of certain items of my tangible personal property. Any such statement or list in existence at the time of my death shall be determinative with respect to all items bequeathed therein.

THIRD: I give, devise, and bequeath all my estate, real, personal, and mixed, of whatever kind and wherever situated, of which I may die seized or possessed, or in which I may have any interest or over which I may have any power of appointment or testamentary disposition, to my children _____

_____

_____,
plus any afterborn or adopted children in equal shares or to their lineal descendants per stirpes.

FOURTH: In the event that any beneficiary fails to survive me by thirty days, then this will shall take effect as if that person had predeceased me.

FIFTH: In the event that any of my children have not reached the age of _____ years at the time of my death, then the share of any such child shall be held in a separate trust by _____ for such child.

The trustee shall use the income and that part of the principal of the trust as is, in the trustee's sole discretion, necessary or desirable to provide proper housing, medical care, food, clothing, entertainment and education for the trust beneficiary, considering the beneficiary's other resources. Any income that is not distributed shall be added to the principal. Additionally, the trustee shall have all powers conferred by the law of the state having jurisdiction over this trust, as well as the power to pay from the assets of the trust reasonable fees necessary to administer the trust.

The trust shall terminate when the child reaches the age specified above and the remaining assets distributed to the child, unless they have been exhausted sooner. In the event the child dies prior to the termination of the trust, then the assets shall pass to the estate of the child. The interests of the beneficiary under this trust shall not be assignable and shall be free from the claims of creditors to the full extent allowed by law.

In the event the said trustee is unable or unwilling to serve for any reason, then I nominate, constitute, and appoint _____as alternate trustee. No bond shall be required of either trustee in any jurisdiction and this trust shall be administered without court supervision as allowed by law.

Page 1 of ___ pages.

SIXTH: In the event any of my children have not attained the age of 18 years at the time of my death, I hereby nominate, constitute, and appoint _____ as guardian over the person of any of my children who have not reached the age of majority at the time of my death. In the event that said guardian is unable or unwilling to serve, then I nominate, constitute, and appoint _____ as guardian. Said guardian shall serve without bond or surety.

SEVENTH: I hereby nominate, constitute, and appoint _____ as Personal Representative of this, my Last Will and Testament. In the event that such named person is unable or unwilling to serve at any time or for any reason, then I nominate, constitute, and appoint _____ as Personal Representative in the place and stead of the person first named herein. It is my will and I direct that my Personal Representative shall not be required to furnish a bond for the faithful performance of his or her duties in any jurisdiction, any provision of law to the contrary notwithstanding, and I give my Personal Representative full power to administer my estate, including the power to settle claims, pay debts, and sell, lease or exchange real and personal property without court order.

IN WITNESS WHEREOF I have signed and published this Last Will and Testament, consisting of two pages, this _____ day of _____, _____.

_____

## STATEMENT OF WITNESSES

We sign below as witnesses, declaring that the person who is making this will appears to be of sound mind and appears to be making this will freely and without duress, fraud, or undue influence and that the person making this will acknowledges that he or she has read, or has had it read to them, and understands the contents of this will.

_____  
(Signature of Witness)

_____  
(Signature of Witness)

_____  
(Print Name)

_____  
(Print Name)

_____  
(Address)

_____  
(Address)

_____  
(City)    (State)    (Zip)

_____  
(City)    (State)    (Zip)

# Last Will and Testament

I, _____ a resident of _____ County, Michigan, declare this to be my will, hereby revoking any prior wills and codicils.

**FIRST:** I direct that all my debts and funeral expenses be paid out of my estate as soon after my death as is practicable.

**SECOND:** I may leave a separate statement or list disposing of certain items of my tangible personal property. Any such statement or list in existence at the time of my death shall be determinative with respect to all items bequeathed therein.

**THIRD:** I give, devise, and bequeath all my estate, real, personal, and mixed, of whatever kind and wherever situated, of which I may die seized or possessed, or in which I may have any interest or over which I may have any power of appointment or testamentary disposition, to my children _____
_____, in equal shares, or their lineal descendants per stirpes.

**FOURTH:** In the event that any beneficiary fails to survive me by thirty days, then this will shall take effect as if that person had predeceased me.

**FIFTH:** I hereby nominate, constitute, and appoint _____ as Personal Representative of this, my Last Will and Testament. In the event that such named person is unable or unwilling to serve at any time or for any reason, then I nominate, constitute, and appoint _____ as Personal Representative in the place and stead of the person first named herein. It is my will and I direct that my Personal Representative shall not be required to furnish a bond for the faithful performance of his or her duties in any jurisdiction, any provision of law to the contrary notwithstanding, and I give my Personal Representative full power to administer my estate, including the power to settle claims, pay debts, and sell, lease or exchange real and personal property without court order.

IN WITNESS WHEREOF I have signed and published this Last Will and Testament, consisting of two pages, this _____ day of _____, _____.

_____

## STATEMENT OF WITNESSES

We sign below as witnesses, declaring that the person who is making this will appears to be of sound mind and appears to be making this will freely and without duress, fraud, or undue influence and that the person making this will acknowledges that he or she has read, or has had it read to them, and understands the contents of this will.

| _____ | | | _____ | | |
| (Signature of Witness) | | | (Signature of Witness) | | |
| _____ | | | _____ | | |
| (Print Name) | | | (Print Name) | | |
| _____ | | | _____ | | |
| (Address) | | | (Address) | | |
| _____ | _____ | _____ | _____ | _____ | _____ |
| (City) | (State) | (Zip) | (City) | (State) | (Zip) |

# Last Will and Testament

I, _____ a resident of _____ County, Michigan, declare this to be my will, hereby revoking any prior wills and codicils.

**FIRST:** I direct that all my debts and funeral expenses be paid out of my estate as soon after my death as is practicable.

**SECOND:** I may leave a separate statement or list disposing of certain items of my tangible personal property. Any such statement or list in existence at the time of my death shall be determinative with respect to all items bequeathed therein.

**THIRD:** I give, devise, and bequeath all my estate, real, personal, and mixed, of whatever kind and wherever situated, of which I may die seized or possessed, or in which I may have any interest or over which I may have any power of appointment or testamentary disposition, to my children_____ _____, in equal shares, or their lineal descendants per capita.

**FOURTH:** In the event that any beneficiary fails to survive me by thirty days, then this will shall take effect as if that person had predeceased me.

**FIFTH:** I hereby nominate, constitute, and appoint _____ as Personal Representative of this, my Last Will and Testament. In the event that such named person is unable or unwilling to serve at any time or for any reason, then I nominate, constitute, and appoint _____ as Personal Representative in the place and stead of the person first named herein. It is my will and I direct that my Personal Representative shall not be required to furnish a bond for the faithful performance of his or her duties in any jurisdiction, any provision of law to the contrary notwithstanding, and I give my Personal Representative full power to administer my estate, including the power to settle claims, pay debts, and sell, lease or exchange real and personal property without court order.

**IN WITNESS WHEREOF** I have signed and published this Last Will and Testament, consisting of two pages, this _____ day of _____, _____.

_____

## STATEMENT OF WITNESSES

We sign below as witnesses, declaring that the person who is making this will appears to be of sound mind and appears to be making this will freely and without duress, fraud, or undue influence and that the person making this will acknowledges that he or she has read, or has had it read to them, and understands the contents of this will.

| | |
|---|---|
| _____ | _____ |
| (Signature of Witness) | (Signature of Witness) |
| _____ | _____ |
| (Print Name) | (Print Name) |
| _____ | _____ |
| (Address) | (Address) |
| _____ _____ _____ | _____ _____ _____ |
| (City)      (State)      (Zip) | (City)      (State)      (Zip) |

# Last Will and Testament
# of

_____

I, _____ a resident of _____ County, Michigan, declare this to be my will, hereby revoking any prior wills and codicils.

FIRST: I direct that all my debts and funeral expenses be paid out of my estate as soon after my death as is practicable.

SECOND: I may leave a separate statement or list disposing of certain items of my tangible personal property. Any such statement or list in existence at the time of my death shall be determinative with respect to all items bequeathed therein.

THIRD: I give, devise, and bequeath all my estate, real, personal, and mixed, of whatever kind and wherever situated, of which I may die seized or possessed, or in which I may have any interest or over which I may have any power of appointment or testamentary disposition, to the following:

_____

_____

_____

_____

_____

_____,

or to the survivor of them.

FOURTH: In the event that any beneficiary fails to survive me by thirty days, then this will shall take effect as if that person had predeceased me.

FIFTH: I hereby nominate, constitute, and appoint _____ as Personal Representative of this, my Last Will and Testament. In the event that such named person is unable or unwilling to serve at any time or for any reason, then I nominate, constitute, and appoint _____ as Personal Representative in the place and stead of the person first named herein. It is my will and I direct that my Personal Representative shall not be required to furnish a bond for the faithful performance of his or her duties in any jurisdiction, any provision of law to the contrary notwithstanding, and I give my Personal Representative full power to administer my estate, including the power to settle claims, pay debts, and sell, lease or exchange real and personal property without court order.

Page 1 of ___ pages.

**IN WITNESS WHEREOF** I have signed and published this Last Will and Testament, consisting of two pages, this _____ day of _____, _____.

_____

STATEMENT OF WITNESSES

We sign below as witnesses, declaring that the person who is making this will appears to be of sound mind and appears to be making this will freely and without duress, fraud, or undue influence and that the person making this will acknowledges that he or she has read, or has had it read to them, and understands the contents of this will.

_____      _____
(Print Name)                    (Signature of Witness)

_____
(Address)

_____
(City)     (State)     (Zip)

_____      _____
(Print Name)                    (Signature of Witness)

_____
(Address)

_____
(City)     (State)     (Zip)

Page 2 of ___ pages.

# Last Will and Testament
## of

_____

I, _____ a resident of _____ County, Michigan, declare this to be my will, hereby revoking any prior wills and codicils.

FIRST: I direct that all my debts and funeral expenses be paid out of my estate as soon after my death as is practicable.

SECOND: I may leave a separate statement or list disposing of certain items of my tangible personal property. Any such statement or list in existence at the time of my death shall be determinative with respect to all items bequeathed therein.

THIRD: I give, devise, and bequeath all my estate, real, personal, and mixed, of whatever kind and wherever situated, of which I may die seized or possessed, or in which I may have any interest or over which I may have any power of appointment or testamentary disposition, to the following:

_____

_____

_____

_____

_____

_____,

in equal shares, or their lineal descendants per stirpes.

FOURTH: In the event that any beneficiary fails to survive me by thirty days, then this will shall take effect as if that person had predeceased me.

FIFTH: I hereby nominate, constitute, and appoint _____ as Personal Representative of this, my Last Will and Testament. In the event that such named person is unable or unwilling to serve at any time or for any reason, then I nominate, constitute, and appoint _____ as Personal Representative in the place and stead of the person first named herein. It is my will and I direct that my Personal Representative shall not be required to furnish a bond for the faithful performance of his or her duties in any jurisdiction, any provision of law to the contrary notwithstanding, and I give my Personal Representative full power to administer my estate, including the power to settle claims, pay debts, and sell, lease or exchange real and personal property without court order.

Page 1 of ___ pages.

**IN WITNESS WHEREOF** I have signed and published this Last Will and Testament, consisting of two pages, this _____ day of _____, _____.

_____

## STATEMENT OF WITNESSES

    We sign below as witnesses, declaring that the person who is making this will appears to be of sound mind and appears to be making this will freely and without duress, fraud, or undue influence and that the person making this will acknowledges that he or she has read, or has had it read to them, and understands the contents of this will.

_____      _____
(Print Name)                                (Signature of Witness)

_____
(Address)

_____
(City)         (State)        (Zip)

_____      _____
(Print Name)                                (Signature of Witness)

_____
(Address)

_____
(City)         (State)        (Zip)

Page 2 of ____ pages.

STATE OF MICHIGAN

COUNTY OF _____

      We, _____, the testator, and

_____, and _____, the witnesses, whose names are signed to the attached or foregoing instrument and whose signatures appear below, having been duly sworn, declared to the undersigned officer that: 1) the attached or foregoing instrument is the last will of the testator; 2) the testator willingly and voluntarily declared, signed, and executed the will in the presence of the witnesses; 3) the witnesses signed the will upon the request of the testator, in the presence and hearing of the testator and in the presence of each other; 4) to the best knowledge of each witness, the testator was, at the time of signing, of the age of majority (or otherwise legally competent to make a will), of sound mind and memory, and under no constraint, duress, fraud, or undue influence; 5) the testator acknowledged that he or she has read this will, or has had it read to him or her, and understands the contents of this will; and 6) each witness was and is competent and of proper age to witness a will.

_____ (Testator)

_____ (Witness)

_____ (Witness)

Subscribed and sworn to before me by _____, the testator, and by _____ and _____, the witnesses, all of whom personally appeared before me on _____, _____, each of whom is either personally known to me or produced identification as follows:

Name:                        Personally known/Identification

_____      _____

_____      _____

_____      _____

_____

Notary Public
My Commission Expires:

                              Page ___ of ___ pages.

# Codicil to the Will of

_____

I, _____, a resident of _____
County, Michigan, declare this to be the first codicil to my Last Will and Testament dated
_____, _____.

FIRST: I hereby revoke the clause of my Will which reads as follows: _____
_____
_____
_____.

SECOND: I hereby add the following clause to my Will: _____
_____
_____
_____.

THIRD: In all other respects I hereby confirm and republish my Last Will and
Testament dated _____, _____.

IN WITNESS WHEREOF, I have signed and published the foregoing instrument as
and for a codicil to my Last Will and Testament, this _____ day of _____,
_____.

_____

## STATEMENT OF WITNESSES

We sign below as witnesses, declaring that the person who is making this will appears to be of
sound mind and appears to be making this will freely and without duress, fraud, or undue influence
and that the person making this will acknowledges that he or she has read, or has had it read to them,
and understands the contents of this will.

| _____ | _____ |
| (Signature of Witness) | (Signature of Witness) |
| _____ | _____ |
| (Print Name) | (Print Name) |
| _____ | _____ |
| (Address) | (Address) |
| (City)      (State)      (Zip) | (City)      (State)      (Zip) |

STATE OF MICHIGAN

COUNTY OF _____

  We, _____, the testator, and
_____, and _____,
the witnesses, whose names are signed to the attached or foregoing instrument and whose
signatures appear below, having been duly sworn, declared to the undersigned officer that:
1) the attached or foregoing instrument is a codicil to the last will of the testator; 2) the testator willingly and voluntarily declared, signed, and executed the codicil in the presence of
the witnesses; 3) the witnesses signed the codicil upon the request of the testator, in the presence and hearing of the testator and in the presence of each other; 4) to the best knowledge
of each witness, the testator was, at the time of signing, of the age of majority (or otherwise
legally competent to make a will), of sound mind and memory, and under no constraint,
duress, fraud, or undue influence; 5) the testator acknowledged that he or she has read this
codicil, or has had it read to him or her, and understands the contents of this codicil; and 6)
each witness was and is competent and of proper age to witness a codicil to a will.

_____ (Testator)

_____ (Witness)

_____ (Witness)

Subscribed and sworn to before me by _____, the testator, and by _____ and _____, the witnesses, all
of whom personally appeared before me on _____, _____,
each of whom is either personally known to me or produced identification as follows:
  Name:            Personally known/Identification:

_____  _____

_____  _____

_____  _____


_____

Notary Public
My Commission Expires:

# Designation of Patient Advocate and Living Will

I, _____, appoint
_____, whose address is
_____ and whose
telephone number is _____, as my patient advocate pursuant to M.S.A.
§27.5496; M.C.L.A. §700.496. I appoint _____,
whose address is _____ and whose
telephone number is _____, as my alternate patient advocate in the event my
patient advocate designated above does not accept the appointment, is incapacitated, or is removed.
I authorize my patient advocate to make health care decisions for me when I am incapable of making my own heath care decisions, including decisions to withhold or withdraw medical treatment, even if such withholding or withdrawal could or would allow me to die. I understand the consequences of appointing a patient advocate.

I direct that my agent comply with the following instructions or limitations:
_____
_____.

I also direct that my patient advocate have authority to make decisions regarding the enforcement of my intentions regarding life-prolonging procedures as stated below:

I, _____, being of
sound mind willfully and voluntarily make known my desire that my dying shall not be artificially prolonged under the circumstances set forth below, do hereby declare:

If I should have an incurable or irreversible condition that will cause my death within a relatively short time, and if I am unable to make decisions regarding my medical treatment, I direct my attending physician to withhold or withdraw procedures that merely prolong the dying process and are not necessary to my comfort, or to alleviate pain.

This authorization [check only one box] ❑ includes   ❑ does not include   the withholding or withdrawal of artificial feeding and hydration.

Signed this _____ day of _____, _____.

_____
Signature
Address:_____
_____

The declarant is personally known to me and voluntarily signed this document in my presence.

Witness:_____       Witness:_____
Name:_____       Name:_____
Address:_____       Address:_____
_____                 _____

## Acceptance of Patient Advocate

I HEREBY accept the appointment as patient advocate and understand that:

(a) This designation shall not become effective unless the patient is unable to participate in medical decisions.

(b) A patient advocate shall not exercise powers concerning the patient's care, custody, and medical treatment that the patient, if the patient were able to participate in the decision, could not have exercised on his or her own behalf.

(c) This designation cannot be used to make a medical treatment decision to withhold or withdraw treatment from a patient who is pregnant that would result in the pregnant patient's death.

(d) A patient advocate may make a decision to withhold or withdraw treatment which would allow a patient to die only if the patient has expressed in a clear and convincing manner that the patient advocate is authorized to make such a decision, and that the patient acknowledges that such a decision could or would allow the patient's death.

(e) A patient advocate shall not receive compensation for the performance of his or her authority, rights, and responsibilities, but a patient advocate may be reimbursed for actual and necessary expenses incurred in the performance of his or her authority, rights, and responsibilities.

(f) A patient advocate shall act in accordance with the standards of care applicable to fiduciaries when acting for the patient and shall act consistent with the patient's best interests. The known desires of the patient expressed or evidenced while the patient is able to participate in medical treatment decisions are presumed to be in the patient's best interests.

(g) A patient may revoke his or her designation at any time and in any manner sufficient to communicate an intent to revoke.

(h) A patient advocate may revoke his or her acceptance to the designation at any time and in any manner sufficient to communicate an intent to revoke.

(i) A patient admitted to a health facility or agency has the rights enumerated in section 20201 of the public health code, Act No. 368 of the Public Acts of 1978, being section 33.20201 of the Michigan Compiled Laws.

Date: _____

_____
Signature

## UNIFORM DONOR CARD

The undersigned hereby makes this anatomical gift, if medically acceptable, to take effect on death. The words and marks below indicate my desires:

I give:    (a) \_\_\_\_ any needed organs or parts;

         (b) \_\_\_\_ only the following organs or parts

_____

for the purpose of transplantation, therapy, medical research, or education;

         (c) \_\_\_\_ my body for anatomical study if needed.

Limitations or special wishes, if any:

_____

_____

Signed by the donor and the following witnesses in the presence of each other:

_____  _____
Signature of Donor        Date of birth

_____  _____
Date signed         City & State

_____  _____
Witness         Witness

_____  _____
Address         Address

## UNIFORM DONOR CARD

The undersigned hereby makes this anatomical gift, if medically acceptable, to take effect on death. The words and marks below indicate my desires:

I give:    (a) \_\_\_\_ any needed organs or parts;

         (b) \_\_\_\_ only the following organs or parts

_____

for the purpose of transplantation, therapy, medical research, or education;

         (c) \_\_\_\_ my body for anatomical study if needed.

Limitations or special wishes, if any:

_____

_____

Signed by the donor and the following witnesses in the presence of each other:

_____  _____
Signature of Donor        Date of birth

_____  _____
Date signed         City & State

_____  _____
Witness         Witness

_____  _____
Address         Address

## UNIFORM DONOR CARD

The undersigned hereby makes this anatomical gift, if medically acceptable, to take effect on death. The words and marks below indicate my desires:

I give:    (a) \_\_\_\_ any needed organs or parts;

         (b) \_\_\_\_ only the following organs or parts

_____

for the purpose of transplantation, therapy, medical research, or education;

         (c) \_\_\_\_ my body for anatomical study if needed.

Limitations or special wishes, if any:

_____

_____

Signed by the donor and the following witnesses in the presence of each other:

_____  _____
Signature of Donor        Date of birth

_____  _____
Date signed         City & State

_____  _____
Witness         Witness

_____  _____
Address         Address

## UNIFORM DONOR CARD

The undersigned hereby makes this anatomical gift, if medically acceptable, to take effect on death. The words and marks below indicate my desires:

I give:    (a) \_\_\_\_ any needed organs or parts;

         (b) \_\_\_\_ only the following organs or parts

_____

for the purpose of transplantation, therapy, medical research, or education;

         (c) \_\_\_\_ my body for anatomical study if needed.

Limitations or special wishes, if any:

_____

_____

Signed by the donor and the following witnesses in the presence of each other:

_____  _____
Signature of Donor        Date of birth

_____  _____
Date signed         City & State

_____  _____
Witness         Witness

_____  _____
Address         Address

One of these cards should be cut out and carried in your wallet or purse.  **115**

# GLOSSARY

The following is a selection of legal words and phrases, either used in this book or which you may encounter in research or discussing wills with a lawyer or others. Other terms are defined throughout this book. If you can't find the word you are looking for here, check for it in the index.

**administrator (administratrix** if female). A person appointed by the court to oversee distribution of the property of someone who died (either without a will, or if the person designated in the will is unable to serve). However, in Michigan today, this person is called a *personal representative*.

**beneficiary.** A person who is entitled to receive property from a person who died (regardless of whether there is a will).

**bequest.** Personal property left to someone in a will.

**codicil.** A change or amendment to a will.

**decedent.** A person who has died.

**descendant.** A child, grandchild, great-grandchild, etc.

**devise.** Real property left to someone in a will. A person who is entitled to a devise is called a *devisee.*

**elective share.** The portion of the estate which may be taken by a surviving spouse, regardless of what the will says.

**executor (executrix** if female). A person appointed in a will to oversee distribution of the property of someone who died with a will. However, in Michigan today, this person is called a *personal representative.*

**exempt property.** Property which is exempt from distribution as a normal part of the estate.

**family allowance.** An amount of money set aside from the estate to support the family of the decedent for a period of time.

**forced share.** See *elective share.*

**heir.** A person who will inherit from a decedent who died without a will.

**intestate.** Without making a will. One who dies without a will is said to have *died intestate.*

**intestate share.** The portion of the estate a spouse is entitled to receive if there is no will. In Michigan, this portion varies from one-half to all of the estate, depending upon whether the decedent had any children.

**joint tenancy.** A type of property ownership by two or more persons, in which if one owner dies, that owner's interest goes to the other joint tenants (not to the deceased owner's heirs as in tenancy in common).

**legacy.** Real property left to someone in a will. A person who is entitled to a legacy is called a *legatee.*

**living will.** A document expressing the writer's desires regarding how medical care is to be handled in the event the writer is not able to express his or her wishes concerning the use of life-prolonging medical procedures.

**personal representative.** A person appointed by the court, or will, to oversee distribution of the property of the person who died. This is a more modern term than "administrator," "executor," etc., and applies regardless of whether there is a will.

**probate.** The process of settling a decedent's estate through the probate court.

**residue.** The property that is left over in an estate after all specific bequests and devises.

**specific bequest** or **specific devise.** A gift in a will of a specific item of property, or a specific amount of cash.

**tenancy by the entireties.** A type of property ownership by a married couple. This is generally the same as joint tenancy, except that it is only between a husband and wife.

**tenancy in common.** Ownership of property by two of more people, in which each owner's share would descend to that owner's heirs (not to the other owners as in joint tenancy).

**testate.** With a will. One who dies with a will is said to have "died testate."

**testator.** (**testatrix** if female.) A person who makes his or her will.

# INDEX

*Your #1 Source for Real World Legal Information...*

# SPHINX® PUBLISHING
## A Division of Sourcebooks, Inc.®

- Written by lawyers
- Simple English explanation of the law
- Forms and instructions included

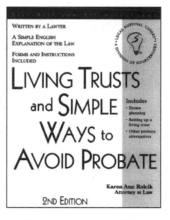

### HOW TO WRITE YOUR OWN PREMARITAL AGREEMENT, (2E)

A premarital agreement can go hand-in-hand with a will and other estate planning measures to enable you, not the government, to control your property upon death. This book includes a state-by-state summary of inheritance and divorce laws, and forms.

180 pages; $19.95;
ISBN 1-57071-344-8

### HOW TO WRITE YOUR OWN LIVING WILL

In a traumatic situation, the decision of life support could be very difficult for a family member to make. Make your wishes known ahead of time by using this step-by-step guide for writing living wills in all 50 states and the District of Columbia. Complete with necessary forms.

148 pages; $9.95;
ISBN 1-57071-167-4

### LIVING TRUSTS & SIMPLE WAYS TO AVOID PROBATE, (2E)

Passing your estate on to your family or heirs can be an expensive, time-consuming process if you are forced to go through today's probate court systems. This book explains everything you need to know to successfully avoid common costs and delays in passing on your property.

160 pages; $19.95;
ISBN 1-57071-336-7

### OTHER MICHIGAN LEGAL SURVIVAL GUIDES

| | |
|---|---|
| How to File for Divorce in MI, 2nd ed. | $19.95 |
| How to Start a Business in MI, 2nd ed. | $16.95 |

SEE OUR ORDER FORM FOR BOOKS WRITTEN FOR OTHER STATES. COMING SOON: OHIO AND NEW JERSEY!

### WHAT OUR CUSTOMERS SAY ABOUT OUR BOOKS:

"Your real estate contracts book has saved me nearly $12,000.00 in closing costs over the past year." —A.B.

"...many of the legal questions that I have had over the years were answered clearly and concisely through your plain English interpretation of the law." —C.E.H.

"If there weren't people out there like you I'd be lost. You have the best books of this type out there." —S.B

*Legal Survival Guides are directly available from Sourcebooks, Inc., or from your local bookstores.*
*For credit card orders call 1–800–43–BRIGHT, write P.O. Box 372, Naperville, IL 60566,*
*or fax 630-961-2168*

# SPHINX® PUBLISHING'S NATIONAL TITLES
*Valid in All 50 States*

## LEGAL SURVIVAL IN BUSINESS

| | |
|---|---|
| How to Form Your Own Corporation (2E) | $19.95 |
| How to Form Your Own Partnership | $19.95 |
| How to Register Your Own Copyright (2E) | $19.95 |
| How to Register Your Own Trademark (2E) | $19.95 |
| Most Valuable Business Legal Forms You'll Ever Need (2E) | $19.95 |
| Most Valuable Corporate Forms You'll Ever Need (2E) | $24.95 |
| Software Law (with diskette) | $29.95 |

## LEGAL SURVIVAL IN COURT

| | |
|---|---|
| Crime Victim's Guide to Justice | $19.95 |
| Debtors' Rights (3E) | $12.95 |
| Defend Yourself Against Criminal Charges | $19.95 |
| Grandparents' Rights | $19.95 |
| Help Your Lawyer Win Your Case | $12.95 |
| Jurors' Rights (2E) | $9.95 |
| Legal Malpractice and Other Claims Against Your Lawyer | $18.95 |
| Legal Research Made Easy (2E) | $14.95 |
| Simple Ways to Protect Yourself From Lawsuits | $24.95 |
| Victims' Rights | $12.95 |
| Winning Your Personal Injury Claim | $19.95 |

## LEGAL SURVIVAL IN REAL ESTATE

| | |
|---|---|
| How to Buy a Condominium or Townhome | $16.95 |
| How to Negotiate Real Estate Contracts (3E) | $16.95 |
| How to Negotiate Real Estate Leases (3E) | $16.95 |
| Successful Real Estate Brokerage Management | $19.95 |

## LEGAL SURVIVAL IN PERSONAL AFFAIRS

| | |
|---|---|
| How to File Your Own Bankruptcy (4E) | $19.95 |
| How to File Your Own Divorce (3E) | $19.95 |
| How to Make Your Own Will | $12.95 |
| How to Write Your Own Living Will | $9.95 |
| How to Write Your Own Premarital Agreement (2E) | $19.95 |
| How to Win Your Unemployment Compensation Claim | $19.95 |
| Living Trusts and Simple Ways to Avoid Probate (2E) | $19.95 |
| Most Valuable Personal Legal Forms You'll Ever Need | $14.95 |
| Neighbor vs. Neighbor | $12.95 |
| The Power of Attorney Handbook (3E) | $19.95 |
| Simple Ways to Protect Yourself from Lawsuits | $24.95 |
| Social Security Benefits Handbook (2E) | $14.95 |
| Unmarried Parents' Rights | $19.95 |
| U.S.A. Immigration Guide (3E) | $19.95 |
| Guia de Inmigracion a Estados Unidos | $19.95 |

*Legal Survival Guides are directly available from Sourcebooks, Inc., or from your local bookstores.*

*For credit card orders call 1–800–43–BRIGHT, write P.O. Box 372, Naperville, IL 60566, or fax 630-961-2168*

# SPHINX® PUBLISHING ORDER FORM

| BILL TO: | | | SHIP TO: | | |
|---|---|---|---|---|---|
| | | | | | |
| | | | | | |
| Phone # | | Terms | F.O.B. Chicago, IL | Ship Date | |

**Charge my:** ☐ VISA   ☐ MasterCard   ☐ American Express

☐ **Money Order or Personal Check**

Credit Card Number      Expiration Date

| Qty | ISBN | Title | Retail | Ext. |
|---|---|---|---|---|
| | | **SPHINX PUBLISHING NATIONAL TITLES** | | |
| | 1-57071-166-6 | Crime Victim's Guide to Justice | $19.95 | |
| | 1-57071-342-1 | Debtors' Rights (3E) | $12.95 | |
| | 1-57071-162-3 | Defend Yourself against Criminal Charges | $19.95 | |
| | 1-57248-001-7 | Grandparents' Rights | $19.95 | |
| | 0-913825-99-9 | Guia de Inmigracion a Estados Unidos | $19.95 | |
| | 1-57248-021-1 | Help Your Lawyer Win Your Case | $12.95 | |
| | 1-57071-164-X | How to Buy a Condominium or Townhome | $16.95 | |
| | 1-57071-223-9 | How to File Your Own Bankruptcy (4E) | $19.95 | |
| | 1-57071-224-7 | How to File Your Own Divorce (3E) | $19.95 | |
| | 1-57071-227-1 | How to Form Your Own Corporation (2E) | $19.95 | |
| | 1-57071-343-X | How to Form Your Own Partnership | $19.95 | |
| | 1-57071-228-X | How to Make Your Own Will | $12.95 | |
| | 1-57071-331-6 | How to Negotiate Real Estate Contracts (3E) | $16.95 | |
| | 1-57071-332-4 | How to Negotiate Real Estate Leases (3E) | $16.95 | |
| | 1-57071-225-5 | How to Register Your Own Copyright (2E) | $19.95 | |
| | 1-57071-226-3 | How to Register Your Own Trademark (2E) | $19.95 | |
| | 1-57071-349-9 | How to Win Your Unemployment Compensation Claim | $19.95 | |
| | 1-57071-167-4 | How to Write Your Own Living Will | $9.95 | |
| | 1-57071-344-8 | How to Write Your Own Premarital Agreement (2E) | $19.95 | |
| | 1-57071-333-2 | Jurors' Rights (2E) | $9.95 | |
| | 1-57248-032-7 | Legal Malpractice and Other Claims against... | $18.95 | |
| | 1-57071-400-2 | Legal Research Made Easy (2E) | $14.95 | |
| | 1-57071-336-7 | Living Trusts and Simple Ways to Avoid Probate (2E) | $19.95 | |
| | 1-57071-345-6 | Most Valuable Bus. Legal Forms You'll Ever Need (2E) | $19.95 | |
| | 1-57071-346-4 | Most Valuable Corporate Forms You'll Ever Need (2E) | $24.95 | |
| | 1-57071-347-2 | Most Valuable Personal Legal Forms You'll Ever Need | $14.95 | |

| Qty | ISBN | Title | Retail | Ext. |
|---|---|---|---|---|
| | 0-913825-41-7 | Neighbor vs. Neighbor | $12.95 | |
| | 1-57071-348-0 | The Power of Attorney Handbook (3E) | $19.95 | |
| | 1-57248-020-3 | Simple Ways to Protect Yourself from Lawsuits | $24.95 | |
| | 1-57071-337-5 | Social Security Benefits Handbook (2E) | $14.95 | |
| | 1-57071-163-1 | Software Law (w/diskette) | $29.95 | |
| | 0-913825-86-7 | Successful Real Estate Brokerage Mgmt. | $19.95 | |
| | 1-57071-399-5 | Unmarried Parents' Rights | $19.95 | |
| | 1-57071-354-5 | U.S.A. Immigration Guide (3E) | $19.95 | |
| | 0-913825-82-4 | Victims' Rights | $12.95 | |
| | 1-57071-165-8 | Winning Your Personal Injury Claim | $19.95 | |
| | | **CALIFORNIA TITLES** | | |
| | 1-57071-360-X | CA Power of Attorney Handbook | $12.95 | |
| | 1-57071-355-3 | How to File for Divorce in CA | $19.95 | |
| | 1-57071-356-1 | How to Make a CA Will | $12.95 | |
| | 1-57071-408-8 | How to Probate an Estate in CA | $19.95 | |
| | 1-57071-357-X | How to Start a Business in CA | $16.95 | |
| | 1-57071-358-8 | How to Win in Small Claims Court in CA | $14.95 | |
| | 1-57071-359-6 | Landlords' Rights and Duties in CA | $19.95 | |
| | | **FLORIDA TITLES** | | |
| | 1-57071-363-4 | Florida Power of Attorney Handbook (2E) | $12.95 | |
| | 1-57071–403-7 | How to File for Divorce in FL (5E) | $21.95 | |
| | 1-57071-401-0 | How to Form a Partnership in FL | $19.95 | |
| | 1-57248-004-1 | How to Form a Nonprofit Corp. in FL (3E) | $19.95 | |
| | 1-57071-380-4 | How to Form a Corporation in FL (4E) | $19.95 | |
| | 1-57071-361-8 | How to Make a FL Will (5E) | $12.95 | |
| | *Form Continued on Following Page* | | **SUBTOTAL** | |

To order, call Sourcebooks at 1-800-43-BRIGHT or FAX (630)961-2168 (Bookstores, libraries, wholesalers—please call for discount)

# SPHINX® PUBLISHING ORDER FORM

| Qty | ISBN | Title | Retail | Ext. |
|-----|------|-------|--------|------|
| | | **FLORIDA TITLES (CONT'D)** | | |
| ____ | 1-57248-056-4 | How to Modify Your FL Divorce Judgement (3E) | $22.95 | ____ |
| ____ | 1-57071-364-2 | How to Probate an Estate in FL (3E) | $24.95 | ____ |
| ____ | 1-57248-005-X | How to Start a Business in FL (4E) | $16.95 | ____ |
| ____ | 1-57071-362-6 | How to Win in Small Claims Court in FL (6E) | $14.95 | ____ |
| ____ | 1-57071-335-9 | Landlords' Rights and Duties in FL (7E) | $19.95 | ____ |
| ____ | 1-57071-334-0 | Land Trusts in FL (5E) | $24.95 | ____ |
| ____ | 0-913825-73-5 | Women's Legal Rights in FL | $19.95 | ____ |
| | | **GEORGIA TITLES** | | |
| ____ | 1-57071-387-1 | How to File for Divorce in GA (3E) | $19.95 | ____ |
| ____ | 1-57248-075-0 | How to Make a GA Will (3E) | $12.95 | ____ |
| ____ | 1-57248-076-9 | How to Start a Business in Georgia | $16.95 | ____ |
| | | **ILLINOIS TITLES** | | |
| ____ | 1-57071-405-3 | How to File for Divorce in IL (2E) | $19.95 | ____ |
| ____ | 1-57071-415-0 | How to Make an IL Will (2E) | $12.95 | ____ |
| ____ | 1-57071-416-9 | How to Start a Business in IL (2E) | $16.95 | ____ |
| | | **MASSACHUSETTS TITLES** | | |
| ____ | 1-57071-329-4 | How to File for Divorce in MA (2E) | $19.95 | ____ |
| ____ | 1-57248-050-5 | How to Make a MA Will | $9.95 | ____ |
| ____ | 1-57248-053-X | How to Probate an Estate in MA | $19.95 | ____ |
| ____ | 1-57248-054-8 | How to Start a Business in MA | $16.95 | ____ |
| ____ | 1-57248-055-6 | Landlords' Rights and Duties in MA | $19.95 | ____ |
| | | **MICHIGAN TITLES** | | |
| ____ | 1-57071-409-6 | How to File for Divorce in MI (2E) | $19.95 | ____ |
| ____ | 1-57248-077-7 | How to Make a MI Will (2E) | $12.95 | ____ |
| ____ | 1-57071-407-X | How to Start a Business in MI (2E) | $16.95 | ____ |
| | | **MINNESOTA TITLES** | | |
| ____ | 1-57248-039-4 | How to File for Divorce in MN | $19.95 | ____ |
| ____ | 1-57248-040-8 | How to Form a Simple Corporation in MN | $19.95 | ____ |
| ____ | 1-57248-037-8 | How to Make a MN Will | $9.95 | ____ |
| ____ | 1-57248-038-6 | How to Start a Business in MN | $16.95 | ____ |
| | | **NEW YORK TITLES** | | |
| ____ | 1-57071-184-4 | How to File for Divorce in NY | $19.95 | ____ |
| ____ | 1-57071-183-6 | How to Make a NY Will | $12.95 | ____ |
| ____ | 1-57071-185-2 | How to Start a Business in NY | $16.95 | ____ |
| ____ | 1-57071-187-9 | How to Win in Small Claims Court in NY | $14.95 | ____ |
| ____ | 1-57071-186-0 | Landlords' Rights and Duties in NY | $19.95 | ____ |
| ____ | 1-57071-188-7 | New York Power of Attorney Handbook | $19.95 | ____ |
| | | **NORTH CAROLINA TITLES** | | |
| ____ | 1-57071-326-X | How to File for Divorce in NC (2E) | $19.95 | ____ |
| ____ | 1-57071-327-8 | How to Make a NC Will (2E) | $12.95 | ____ |
| ____ | 0-913825-93-X | How to Start a Business in NC | $16.95 | ____ |
| | | **PENNSYLVANIA TITLES** | | |
| ____ | 1-57071-177-1 | How to File for Divorce in PA | $19.95 | ____ |
| ____ | 1-57071-176-3 | How to Make a PA Will | $12.95 | ____ |
| ____ | 1-57071-178-X | How to Start a Business in PA | $16.95 | ____ |
| ____ | 1-57071-179-8 | Landlords' Rights and Duties in PA | $19.95 | ____ |
| | | **TEXAS TITLES** | | |
| ____ | 1-57071-330-8 | How to File for Divorce in TX (2E) | $19.95 | ____ |
| ____ | 1-57248-009-2 | How to Form a Simple Corporation in TX | $19.95 | ____ |
| ____ | 1-57071-417-7 | How to Make a TX Will (2E) | $12.95 | ____ |
| ____ | 1-57071-418-5 | How to Probate an Estate in TX (2E) | $19.95 | ____ |
| ____ | 1-57071-365-0 | How to Start a Business in TX (2E) | $16.95 | ____ |
| ____ | 1-57248-012-2 | How to Win in Small Claims Court in TX | $14.95 | ____ |
| ____ | 1-57248-011-4 | Landlords' Rights and Duties in TX | $19.95 | ____ |

**SUBTOTAL THIS PAGE** ____

**SUBTOTAL PREVIOUS PAGE** ____

Illinois residents add 6.75% sales tax

Florida residents add 6% state sales tax plus applicable discretionary surtax ____

Shipping— $4.00 for 1st book, $1.00 each additional ____

**TOTAL** ____